Presented To:

_____

From:

_____

Date:

_____

Other Nori Media Books and Movies
by Jim Stovall

The Ultimate Gift
The Ultimate Life
The Ultimate Journey
The Ultimate Legacy
The Millionaire Map
The Ultimate Financial Plan
Ultimate Hindsight
The Gift of a Legacy
A Christmas Snow
Success Secrets of Super Achievers
Today's the Day!
The Art of Learning and Self-Development
The Art of Productivity
The Art of Presentation
The Art of Communication
The Financial Crossroads
Ultimate Productivity
Keeper of the Flame
The Lamp
Poems, Quotes, and Things to Think About
Wisdom of the Ages
Discovering Joye
Top of the Hill
One Season of Hope
Wisdom for Winners Volumes 1, 2, 3, 4
100 Worst Employees
Will to Win
The Gift of Giving
Dear Napoleon

THE ART OF
ENTREPRENEURSHIP

The Proactive Method to
Turn the Time, Talent, & Resources
You Have into What You Want

JIM STOVALL &
DR. KEVIN SCHNEIDER

Published and distributed by:
SOUND WISDOM
P.O. Box 310
Shippensburg, PA 17257-0310

717-530-2122
info@soundwisdom.com
www.soundwisdom.com

While efforts have been made to verify information contained in this publication, neither the author nor the publisher assumes any responsibility for errors, inaccuracies, or omissions. While this publication is chock-full of useful, practical information; it is not intended to be legal or accounting advice. All readers are advised to seek competent lawyers and accountants to follow laws and regulations that may apply to specific situations. The reader of this publication assumes responsibility for the use of the information. The author and publisher assume no responsibility or liability whatsoever on the behalf of the reader of this publication. The scanning, uploading and distribution of this publication via the Internet or via any other means without the permission of the publisher is illegal and punishable by law. Please purchase only authorized editions and do not participate in or encourage piracy of copyrightable materials.

Cover design by Eileen Rockwell
Interior design by Terry Clifton

ISBN 13 TP: 978-1-64095-345-1
ISBN 13 eBook: 978-1-64095-346-8

For Worldwide Distribution, Printed in the U.S.A.
2 3 4 5 6 7 8 / 26 25 24 23 22

DEDICATIONS

This book is dedicated to my wife, Crystal, for being there with me on every step of the journey; to my colleague Beth Sharp for turning my dictation into a coherent manuscript; and to Dr. Kevin Schneider for being my co-author, colleague, collaborator, and friend.

JIM STOVALL, 2021

I would like to dedicate this book to my faithful and loving wife who is a deep well of encouragement and grace and has been a pillar of strength in our marriage; to my children whose laughter and love bring joy to my life; and to my co-author, mentor, and friend Jim Stovall whose wisdom and generosity have so greatly impacted my life.

DR. KEVIN SCHNEIDER, 2021

CONTENTS

CHAPTER ONE

Considering the Journey

by Jim Stovall

Within these pages, we are undertaking a journey of discovery into the world of entrepreneurship. This is a unique world filled with potential and possibilities. It is much bigger, broader, and grander than you can imagine, but it's not for everyone. In many ways, the most important part of any trip or journey is the contemplations, planning, and preparation that takes place before you even depart. Psychologists tell us that we appreciate, value, and derive more happiness from experiences than from possessions. Memories mean more to us than buying stuff we don't need to try and impress people who don't care. It's much more satisfying in the long term to enjoy a trip to the beach than to buy a new bathing suit.

If we look at entrepreneurship as a journey, we first must determine if becoming an entrepreneur is really what we want to do with our life. I am an optimist and believe that all things are possible. We can have anything in our lives, but we can't have everything. When we say yes to one option, we invariably say no to another possibility.

Stovall's 11th Commandment

After more than forty years of being an entrepreneur, I have benefited greatly from a concept I call "Stovall's 11th Commandment." It simply states, "Thou shalt not kid thyself." If you are contemplating living your life as an entrepreneur, you must become very clear regarding what an entrepreneur is and who are you.

In previous books, syndicated columns, and arena speeches, I have repeatedly made the statement that everyone either is an entrepreneur or derives their income from an entrepreneur. People have objected to my statement by declaring that they work for a large corporation, a nonprofit organization, or the government. While these people certainly do not work directly with an entrepreneur, it's important to realize that every large corporation began as an entrepreneurial venture in the mind of one person. Every nonprofit organization is supported directly or indirectly by the contributions derived from entrepreneurship, and governments collect taxes from the direct or indirect efforts of entrepreneurs.

One of the greatest misconceptions in our society today is the idea of government money. Governments do not have money nor do they create it. They, instead, collect money through taxes on the profits created by entrepreneurs. While it can be argued whether good government policies might help entrepreneurs, there can be no doubt that bad government policies can destroy entrepreneurs. For the most part, the best thing governments can do for entrepreneurship is to stay out of the way. Left to their own creativity and efforts, entrepreneurs will create jobs, profit, solutions, and innovations that will continue to improve people's lives and make the world a better place.

Worth the Struggle

I'm reminded of the parable about a great sculptor creating a magnificent statue of an angel. A bystander asked how the artist could create such an incredible masterpiece from a shapeless block of marble. The sculptor responded, "I simply remove everything that is not the angel, and the masterpiece is revealed. Once you get the debris out of the way, you uncover the treasure inside." Our exploration of entrepreneurship can be undertaken in much the same way. Entrepreneurship is not a get-rich-quick scheme.

Most entrepreneurs work for many months or even years before they see any fruit from their labor. Being an entrepreneur is not a salaried position or a job where you work for hourly wages. As an entrepreneur, you are building a vehicle that will take you where you want to go and generate profits as it serves the wants and needs of people around the world.

One of my mentors, Lee Braxton, helped me understand this as I was struggling as a young entrepreneur building my first vehicle. Many of my friends and college classmates began their careers by landing great jobs working for well-established organizations. They received a regular paycheck, paid vacations, retirement benefits, and many other perks that go along with a corporate position. I, on the other hand, was struggling to get my first venture off the ground. I was working longer hours for no income with only the vague hope of a meaningful profit at some nebulous point in the future.

Mr. Braxton told me to imagine lining up alongside all of my friends and classmates at the edge of a huge field. In this example, our objective was to get a large, heavy iron ball from the start line to the finish line all the way at the other end of the field. As Mr. Braxton explained it to me, all the other participants began their quest by rolling the ball along the ground or picking it up and struggling to carry it a few feet at a time. As they were moving ahead of me, I was still standing at the start line working on my entrepreneurial vehicle— which in this example was a cannon.

As the example progressed, everyone moved far out ahead of me in their quest to get their iron ball to the finish line. To the untrained observer, it appeared that I was making no progress at all. However, at a certain point in time, there came a magical moment when my cannon was completed, and I could place my cannonball in the barrel of the cannon with gun powder and a fuse. Then, in the blink of an eye, the progress made by all of my friends and classmates was totally eclipsed as I lit the fuse, the cannon roared, and my cannonball soared high into the air and flew far beyond the finish line.

No Shortcut to Success

Entrepreneurship can never be confused with a job or standard employment career. However, that doesn't mean that everyone should be an entrepreneur. The idea that entrepreneurs get something for nothing or find the shortcut to success could not be further from the truth. Many people who are toiling away at jobs they do not enjoy may daydream of being an entrepreneur where they can get more money for working less while being their own boss. If you believe this, you are clearly violating the 11th Commandment and you are kidding yourself.

It is not our job within these pages to convince you to be an entrepreneur; but instead, it is our mission to give you an accurate picture of what entrepreneurship means so that you can determine what is right for you. If, after reading the last page of this book, you come to the informed conclusion that entrepreneurship is not for you, we will have fulfilled one of the purposes of this book, and you will have succeeded in making a good life choice.

If you determine you do not want to be an entrepreneur, it doesn't mean that you can't succeed. One of the fastest growing groups of new millionaires is made up of people who have a job and invest regularly in their 401K or other retirement vehicle. Whether you decide to be an entrepreneur or work in an organization created by or funded by an entrepreneur, you can become financially independent and exceed all of your career goals.

My father is one of the greatest men I have ever known. He worked for 57 years for one organization before retiring at age 81. He began his career working in the mail room, and retired as the CEO of one of the divisions of that organization. As an entrepreneur myself, I cannot imagine having a more valuable colleague than my father on your team, but he is the furthest thing you can imagine from being an entrepreneur. My father and countless other talented, dedicated, and gifted individuals commit their efforts to making the entrepreneurial ventures of visionaries become reality.

Changing Lanes

As a young man, my only ambition in life was to be an All-American football player and then move on to make my living in the NFL. Then, one year during a routine physical in preparation for playing another season of football, I was diagnosed with a condition that would cause me to lose my sight. I realized my football career was over, but got to finish my athletic career as a national Olympic weightlifting champion.

As my eyesight faded throughout my twenties, I was able to get my college degree with the help of my soon-to-be wife, Crystal, who read my textbooks to me. As graduation day approached, it seemed like all of my friends and classmates were getting wonderful job offers from recruiters, but no one seemed to have any interest in me—a blind, former football player and weightlifting champion. I remember the day I went to my father's office to tell him I wasn't going to get a job—not thrilling news for any parent—but instead, I was going to become an entrepreneur.

I didn't have any idea what it meant to be an entrepreneur, but it sounded better than doing nothing, which seemed to be my only other alternative at the time. My father listened to me describe my plight, then declared, "Come back tomorrow, and I will give you something." I was excited as I could imagine my father giving me a significant amount of money to launch my entrepreneurial ventures.

The next day I arrived at Dad's office eagerly anticipating my windfall. You can imagine my disappointment when he greeted me with the news that he wasn't going to give me any money. He explained, "I'm going to give you the certain knowledge that if you ever get anything out of this life, you got it on your own."

He went on to explain that he didn't know anything about being an entrepreneur, but he was going to
introduce me to a man who served on the board of the
organization that employed my father throughout his
working life. He told me that Lee Braxton had a third
grade education, dropped out of school, and became a
multimillionaire as an entrepreneur during the Great
Depression. Mr. Braxton gave most of his fortune away
and lived off the earnings of his investments as he vol-
unteered for nonprofit organizations and causes that
mattered to him throughout the remainder of this life. I
cannot imagine any amount of money my father could
have given me that would have been worth as much as
the introduction to Lee Braxton.

The Journey Begins

The first day I met Mr. Braxton, he handed me a large
book entitled, *Think and Grow Rich* by Napoleon Hill.
He asked if my failing eyesight would allow me to read
the book. I explained that it would be slow and difficult.
This didn't seem to bother him, and he concluded our
first meeting by saying, "Read that book and come back
and see me."

I struggled through the book with my failing eyesight and returned several weeks later. When I arrived
for our second meeting, Mr. Braxton asked me questions
about the book and apparently didn't like my answers as
he responded, "Go read it again and come back and see

me." After reading the book a second time, I was still unable to satisfy Mr. Braxton with my grasp of the lessons Napoleon Hill laid out in *Think and Grow Rich*.

I read it a third time, and only then did Mr. Braxton begin teaching me about entrepreneurship, first by explaining what an entrepreneur is not. If you are the kind of person who needs the certainty of a regular paycheck, corporate benefits, and a structured workweek, being an entrepreneur is likely not for you. If you like trading your time for someone else's money in a predictable way, entrepreneurship will not serve you well. If you are discouraged, deterred, or diverted by setbacks or rejection, entrepreneurship is not for you.

But if you have a dream, a vision, or a goal deep inside of you that you cannot get away from; if you have a burning desire to create solutions, opportunities, and value in the lives of others; and if you want to make the world a better place to live and profit in the process, entrepreneurship is the vehicle that will get you to your destination.

Everything, and More

Entrepreneurship has given me everything materially and career-wise I have ever wanted in my life and much more. It has provided a pathway to the mountaintop for me as a broke, scared, blind person that would not have existed any other way. Life, in general, and a successful life in particular, is never straightforward, clear, or easy.

Life isn't fair, and we all deal with obstacles and challenges. My blindness is no better or worse than someone else's disability, divorce, bankruptcy, or career setback. We are all only as big as the smallest thing it takes to divert us from where we should be.

Sometimes our career path, business development, or life in general seems totally chaotic. But then, from time to time, we break out of the clouds as we arrive at a plateau where we can look back along the road and examine where we've been and how we got here. During those times of self-examination and enlightenment, we see a grand design and an order that makes us realize there was no other way we could have succeeded.

Years after Lee Braxton made me read Napoleon Hill's *Think and Grow Rich* three times, and the lessons he taught me from that book made me a multimillionaire entrepreneur, I discovered a bit of order in the chaos. After entrepreneurship had taken me from poverty to prosperity and then to purpose, I wrote a book entitled *The Millionaire Map,* in which I shared many of the principles that Mr. Braxton had shared with me. Don Green, who was the head of The Napoleon Hill Foundation, read my book and called me with a revelation that is still hard to believe to this day. He said, "Jim, did you know that your mentor, Lee Braxton, was Napoleon Hill's best friend?" He went on to tell me that Mr. Braxton had given the eulogy at Napoleon Hill's funeral.

Don sent me a file of letters several inches thick that Lee Braxton and Napoleon Hill had exchanged over three decades. I discovered that obscure, intangible formula presented to me in that book many years ago was a direct line of power and possibility from Napoleon Hill through Lee Braxton to me—and now, through these pages, directly to you. The coincidences, hidden treasures, and serendipity go on and on. Success breeds success. You cannot enrich yourself through entrepreneurship without improving the lives of others.

Eventually with Crystal's help, I made it through college; and with Mr. Braxton's direction, I became a successful entrepreneur. I have always believed we make our living based on what we get, but the quality of our life is based on what we give. Crystal and I committed to giving of the time, information, resources, and money that our entrepreneurial success created.

Commitment

Shortly after we graduated from college, we founded a scholarship that, to date, has provided funding for more than 500 college students from around the world. We have funded buildings, worldwide disaster relief, and have paid off several million dollars in medical debt. One of our most significant projects came out of a ten-dollar commitment.

When I was a sophomore in college, there was a speaker on campus who was involved in a project to provide wells for drinking water in sub-Saharan Africa. After his presentation, the president of the university encouraged the student body of more than 4,000 young people to take up a collection to help the water well project.

While I thought this was a great idea, I quickly realized my entire life savings at that moment amounted to seventeen dollars—consisting of a ten-dollar bill, a five-dollar bill, and two one-dollar bills, which were all in my pocket at that moment. To avoid embarrassment, and in an attempt to do the right thing, I got out one of my one-dollar bills preparing to put it in the basket that was being passed down the aisle.

Then, without warning, the president of the university returned to the podium and said, "Someone here needs to hear this—either give your best and expect the best or keep your money because you will need it." I took a deep breath and did one of the hardest things I have ever done in my life. I put my one-dollar bill back in my pocket, took out my ten-dollar bill, and dropped it in the basket as it passed.

Later, I met Crystal outside the building. I was a bit nervous because we had a date planned that night, and we were not yet a couple. I realized that a seven-dollar date was not going to make much of an impression, but I forged ahead and told Crystal, "I have good news and bad news. The good news is I helped that man with his water wells. The bad news is you and I are getting ready to have a seven-dollar date."

Crystal was very gracious then, as she is today after forty years of marriage. She suggested that we could eat in the dining room on campus and then go for a walk. This seemed to fit within my meager budget, so we had a nice dinner, enjoyed a walk across campus, and ended up in an empty classroom where Crystal asked me a question that changed the course of my life. She asked, "What do you think we are going to do when we get out of school?"

The Vision

Since we had never before referred to ourselves as "we" in any of our conversations, I took this as a very positive sign. Since I could still see a little bit at that time, I rushed up to the marker board at the front of the classroom and started writing as I spoke. I explained that I was going to become an entrepreneur and start a business, and then we would start other businesses after that. I explained how we would become millionaires and then multimillionaires. I declared that I would write a book, and that some of my books would be turned into movies. The last thing I wrote on the board that day was my pledge that someday I would find something I cared about as much as that man cared about the water wells, and I would make a donation of a million dollars.

Just as if it had been in one of my novels or movie scripts, one by one, each thing I had written on the marker board that day came true, except for the last thing I had written involving a one million-dollar gift. More than thirty years later, I was in a board meeting at the university where Crystal and I had attended college. The discussions that morning in the board meeting involved what we thought the university should be doing throughout the coming decade. There were many great ideas presented, and someone proposed that the university should have a school of entrepreneurship where young people from around the world could earn their degree in entrepreneurship and learn how to turn their dreams into a successful business venture.

Throughout that entire summer, the idea of a school for entrepreneurship would not leave me alone; so that fall, I asked the president of the university to come to our home, and I presented him with the concept of the Stovall Center for Entrepreneurship. I told him that if he and the university trustees liked the idea, I would write a check for one million dollars. He came back two weeks later and told me the trustees loved the idea, but they had added some elements to my plan, so it was going to cost two million dollars.

The Vision Realized

There I was, forty years after that declaration to give your best and expect the best, so I agreed to give the first million and half of the second million if the university could match it. They found a suitable donor in one of the leading entrepreneurial families in America, and the Stovall Center for Entrepreneurship was born.

The university did an extensive search for a suitable candidate to become the executive director, and they decided on an impressive gentleman named Dr. Kevin Schneider. They sent me his resume and background information, and I realized he had a stellar academic career coupled with real world experience. I met Dr. Schneider backstage as Crystal and I were prepared to go out into the auditorium to present our initial million-dollar gift.

Dr. Schneider was very gracious and kept wanting to thank us. When I explained that we were not part of the process to make him the executive director, as that decision had come from the university president and board, Dr. Schneider explained, "While I'm grateful for my new position as executive director of the Stovall Center for Entrepreneurship, I am also grateful to you and Crystal for giving me one of your college scholarships years ago when I was a struggling undergrad student."

Instantly the clouds broke, and I saw the grand design emerging from the chaos. Entrepreneurship has given me, and continues to give me, everything I want and more, but it also makes a difference for so many others around the world. Whether you have success or failure, it does not exist in a vacuum. You can't succeed or fail without carrying others on your journey.

This journey of entrepreneurship, like any other trip you will undertake, is made more significant and meaningful based on who you travel with. We all can think of times in our lives when we went on a routine errand to a familiar place but were accompanied by a very special person. The otherwise mundane trip became fun, enlightening, and engaging.

I'm very pleased to have Dr. Kevin Schneider as my co-author on this journey into entrepreneurship. In the odd-numbered chapters, I will be giving you the practical reality of entrepreneurship forged from my own experience. In the even-numbered chapters, Dr. Schneider will be providing you with the research and proven principles that can turn your dreams into reality.

CHAPTER TWO

The Entrepreneurial Mindset

by Dr. Kevin Schneider

What is the secret sauce of successful entrepreneurs? Perhaps you think about those who are incredibly creative, extremely brilliant, or exceptionally well-connected when attempting to answer this question. While each of these factors may lead to entrepreneurial success, studying entrepreneurs often leads to the same key ingredient: the entrepreneurial mindset.

So, what is a mindset? The Webster dictionary defines a mindset as "a habitual or characteristic mental attitude that determines how you lives will interpret and respond to situations." In other words, it is a combination of your thought patterns, beliefs, attitudes, and ultimately how you interpret the world around you.

Napoleon Hill undertook perhaps one of the most extensive studies on personal success. He studied hundreds of successful entrepreneurs over the span of two decades, and his research culminated in one of the greatest business books of all time, *Think & Grow Rich*. In the book, Hill covers the thirteen principles he discovered from his research. Included among the many principles: desire, faith, auto-suggestion, imagination, decision, the brain, and the sixth sense. Collectively, the principles describe a comprehensive mindset that contributed to the success of hundreds of the greatest entrepreneurs in modern history and has impacted the thinking of countless thousands of entrepreneurs who have studied and applied Hill's principles.[1]

The Entrepreneurial Learning Initiative (ELI) defines a mindset as "a cognitive belief system consisting of interrelated beliefs, assumptions, and knowledge that we use to process information, inform our decisions, and guide our behavior." The entrepreneurial mindset is further described as "a *specific* set of beliefs, knowledge, and thought processes that drives entrepreneurial behavior." According to ELI, the entrepreneurial mindset includes characteristics such as belief in one's ability to succeed, intrinsic motivation, action-orientation, resilience, future-focus, curiosity, and creativity.[2]

The Network for Teaching Entrepreneurship (NFTE) developed the Entrepreneurial Mindset Index (EMI) that includes eight core domains including: critical thinking; flexibility and adaptability; communication and collaboration; comfort with risk; initiative and self-reliance; future orientation; opportunity recognition;

and creativity and innovation. In study after study, you will see many variations of these combined elements listed that characterize the entrepreneurial mindset.

In this chapter, we will explore several fundamental characteristics that underpin the entrepreneurial mindset as well as how we can develop this capacity.[3]

Think Inside Out (Think It)

In Simon Sinek's book *Start With Why*, he describes the power of knowing your purpose, your cause, your reason for existence. He rightly points out that most organizations or most people know what they do, and even how they do it, but few know *why* they do what they do. People tend to think, act, and communicate from the outside in, which represents what is easiest to what is most difficult to communicate. However, great leaders and great organizations tend to think, act, and communicate from the inside out.[4]

If I were to speak from the "outside in," I might describe the work I do as simply providing a service or making a product. For example, I could explain that my company provides life insurance and financial products and services including stocks, bonds, mutual funds, annuities, and so forth. Our advisors deliver the highest quality products and service available in the industry, and we work harder than our competitors to manage your assets. While this may sound like a decent value proposition, it is uninspiring, and it does not strike at the heart of *why* the company exists.

On the other hand, listen to how the pitch changes when I take an "inside out" approach. Our company exists to ensure you enjoy peace of mind, financial security, and time to spend with your family and loved ones. We believe you should not lose sleep over making difficult life decisions or have to worry about your financial future, and this is why our advisors provide guidance and advice as you progress through life's ups and downs. You can trust our team to provide customized products, services, and advice that fit your needs, lifestyle, and dreams to ensure your financial well-being for the rest of your life. Now that inspires! Ultimately, people don't buy what we do—they buy why we do it.

Inside-out thinking is intrinsic in nature, which is what ELI also discovered about the entrepreneurial mindset. Entrepreneurs are intrinsically motivated, which means they are in touch with the deeper sense of purpose in life and are able to think, behave, and act from internal motivation instead of some other external impetus. This is similar to the concept of locus of control. Those with an internal locus of control believe they are in control of their destiny and responsible for personal success and failure. Alternatively, those with an external locus of control think that external forces impact personal success or failure and tend to believe in luck or chance.

Entrepreneurs are typically driven by the belief that they can make things happen and control the outcome of their efforts. They think from the inside out and know their *why*.

The Power of Vision (See It)

Sight is the ability to see tangible, or perhaps virtual, images with our eyes while *vision* is the ability to imagine, to dream, to invent with our mind what does not yet exist. Sight is seeing what is immediate. Vision is peering into the future. I have never found a more powerful living example of this reality than in my mentor and friend Jim Stovall. I remember reading his first book, *You Don't Have to be Blind to See,* after I heard him speak at the university I attended as an undergraduate student. Jim is one of the greatest entrepreneurs of his era, but his journey did not start out with fame and fortune.

As a blind person, Jim lost his ability to physically see while he was a university student. However, he later developed a vision that would create an entire new industry that would bring television and movies to the millions of blind and visually impaired through launching his company Narrative Television Network. Although Jim had lost his sight, he had not lost his vision. In fact, I have heard him say that if he had to choose between sight and vision, he would choose vision. There are few other abilities entrepreneurs can develop as powerful as vision, and this is exactly what we see as one of the cornerstones of the entrepreneurial mindset.

Although entrepreneurs tend to be visionary and future-oriented, this does not mean you must be able to *predict* the future to be a great entrepreneur. No visionary, regardless of how brilliant that person is, can accurately predict what will happen in the future. On the contrary. Entrepreneurs have a vision in the form of an idea or dream of *what could be* in the future. It is not that they know the future. Rather, it is that they are able to envision some future reality based upon an idea or dream. So, while visionary entrepreneurs do not have some crystal ball by which they predict the future, they have such a strong a picture or dream of their vision that they actually can *create* the future.

Kevin Plank, founder of Under Armour, is another great example how entrepreneurs leverage the power of vision. As a college football player, Plank was frustrated by the inability of his cotton t-shirt to keep him dry. As a result, he started looking for materials that would stay dry and enhance performance. He originally received inspiration for his vision from the same material as women's lingerie after visiting a local fabric store, and it took many prototypes to design a product he could begin selling. It wasn't that he could predict or fore-cast what might happen next, but he could see a future where athletes would wear apparel like a piece of equip-ment that could enhance performance.

His vision was the driving force that kept the company going when he had exhausted his personal savings and maxed out credit cards to fund growth. Although Plank started his business from his grandmother's basement and sold his first products from his car, he built a multi-billion-dollar company that started with a simple vision to keep athletes dry and enhance their performance.

Believe It

Entrepreneurs must believe they have what it takes to be successful, and this belief is most potent when it is a combination of faith and self-confidence. The scriptures teach us that faith is the assurance of what we hope for; it is the evidence of things we cannot see. Faith is therefore a belief in something that you know to be true but you can't see, yet. It is an inherent certainty that something is possible even though the individual cannot currently prove it. Faith requires conviction, and it is a substance that impacts an individual's state of mind.

For instance, in my research and work among low-income households, I have found there are many underlying causes that contribute to material poverty. However, among the various contributors, often the greatest factor is that an individual simply cannot imagine the possibility of escaping poverty. This is commonly known as the poverty mindset, and it is in direct opposition to the faith required for entrepreneurial success.

In addition to a hefty dose of faith, successful entrepreneurs are also self-confident. People who are self-confident believe they have the skills and ability to make something happen. Entrepreneur Henry Ford said, "If you think you can or you can't, you're right." Think about it. Would you step out to start a company if you didn't have conviction about the idea or believe you have the necessary skills or ability to succeed? Self-confidence is not only an important ingredient for entrepreneurial success, it is also a requirement to get started and stay motivated.

Thankfully self-confidence is not merely something you are born with, and there are many ways to grow in confidence. Knowing yourself and your strengths is a great place to start building self-confidence. Making subtle changes in body language such as pulling your shoulders back, maintaining eye contact, and smiling are also known to boost confidence. Other tips for improving self-confidence include developing a positive attitude, practicing thankfulness, and reducing negative influences. It can also help to set realistic goals, notch small wins, and celebrate big victories.

In *Think & Grow Rich*, Napoleon Hill describes how this combination of faith and self-confidence is required to accumulate riches. As the starting point of building wealth, Hill explains faith gives action to the impulse of thought, and it is the only known antidote for failure. It is also the basis for miracles and phenomena that cannot be rationalized by science. Faith enables you to believe that you will receive what you ask for, and when followed by diligent planning, can result in attainment of your desired goals.

According to Hill, self-confidence results in action that can ultimately produce a desired physical reality. In other words, if faith is the substance or fuel for attaining wealth, then self-confidence is the spark that ignites the engine.[5]

Hill illustrates this idea with the following verses:

> *If you think you are beaten, you are,*
> *If you think you dare not, you don't*
> *If you like to win, but you think you can't,*
> *It is almost certain you won't...*
> *Life's battles don't always go*
> *To the stronger or faster man,*
> *But soon or late the man who wins*
> *Is the man who thinks he can!*[6]

Decisive Action (Do It)

It has often been said that the worst decision is no decision, and procrastination is the enemy of action. In *Think & Grow Rich*, Hill describes that lack of decision was near the top of the list of thirty causes in an analysis of more than 25,000 men and women who had experienced failure. They had fallen prey to procrastination and inaction. They had a habit of reaching decisions slowly, if at all, and then frequently changed decisions. However, among the hundreds of million-aires in his study, Hill found every one of them tended to reach decisions quickly while changing decisions much more slowly.[7]

Today there are many frameworks and techniques from decision-making trees to cost/benefit analysis that can aid the entrepreneur in taking action. One of the simplest yet most effective frameworks is the two-by-two matrix. The diagram includes four quadrants, and each axis represents a decision criterion. Stephen Covey used this diagram to design his time management matrix in *The Seven Habits of Highly Effective People*. In his two-by-two matrix, Covey evaluates whether tasks are important/not important and urgent/not urgent. He encourages his readers to use the framework to focus on planning and identifying priorities that are important, reduce tasks that are urgent, and eliminate activities that are not important.[8]

Whether entrepreneurs rely upon a single deci-sion-making framework, or a combination of techniques, they must beware of attempting to "boil the ocean." The idea of boiling the ocean means there is a limited amount of data and time available for making decisions. In other words, there is so much information available today with such a diverse set of variables to the chal-lenges entrepreneurs face, that there is only so much you can know about an issue before making a decision. This does not mean we should not conduct careful analysis and undertake proper due diligence when making decisions. However, the entrepreneur must be aware of how analysis paralysis can impact decision-making.

Relying upon intuition is another way entrepreneurs act decisively in a challenging, fast-paced environment. Intuition is the idea that people can make decisions without using deliberate, analytical reasoning, and it is often referred to as a gut feeling or sixth sense. According to *Psychology Today*, psychologists suggest intuition develops as the mind searches experiences that are stored in our long-term memory. Often referred to as pattern-matching, our brain leverages these past experiences to make future decisions.[9]

A research study published in the *Journal of Psychological Science* was designed to test the existence of intuition. To measure intuition, the scientists used emotional images that were suppressed from the subjects' awareness and studied how effectively they were able to make decisions. Though participants were unaware of the images, the researchers found they were still able to use the unconscious information to improve decision-making. In fact, the study found that intuition can help people make faster, more accurate decisions with greater confidence, and that intuition may be improved with practice.[10]

If you think about it, entrepreneurs use intuition all the time. There are rarely instances where we have perfect information to make a decision. Even if we do have a deluge of accurate data, it does not necessarily tell us what action to take. For instance, billionaire entrepreneur and investor Richard Branson said, "I rely far more on gut instinct than researching huge amounts of statistics." This is not to say we shouldn't review the available data, but we should also not ignore the gut feeling we have when it comes time to make a decision. Barbara Corcoran, real estate mogul and Shark Tank investor, believes strongly in the role of intuition can play and has said, "Don't you dare underestimate the power of your own instinct. Many entrepreneurs who ignore their instinct regret it later."

Learn to Grow (Keep Learning)

In his book *Critical Path*, R. Buckminster Fuller conceived the knowledge doubling curve. Fuller observed that knowledge was doubling around every 100 years until 1900. However, by mid-century, he estimated that knowledge was double every 25 years.[11] Experts estimate knowledge is doubling approximately every year today, and IBM suggests knowledge could eventually double every 12 hours due to rapidly advancing technology such as the "internet of things" and big data.[12] Similarly, the half-life of a professional skill is about five years, which means half of what you learned five years ago is now obsolete.[13]

In today's environment of ever-increasing knowledge and a rapid pace of technological change, successful entrepreneurs must be lifelong learners. This is nothing new for most entrepreneurs, since few know everything they need to know to build a successful company when they get started. When building a new startup from the ground up, most entrepreneurs will tell you they have "no idea" what they are doing.

Alternatively, in a corporate environment where painstaking planning and incremental progress prevail, the idea that you can launch out to do something new without having everything figured out first can seem reckless. Of course, it is not that entrepreneurs are ignorant or less intelligent than their corporate counterparts. Rather, they must have an inner drive for continuous learning to be able to innovate, iterate, and pivot as they launch a new enterprise.

It is important that we have the right mindset if we want to develop the capacity for lifelong learning. Over decades of research, psychologist and professor Carol Dweck has found that a person's mindset is the single most important factor in determining whether or not that person is successful. Dweck's concept of the different mindsets came out of her research regarding how people handle failure, and her research studies illustrate the power of how peoples' mindsets impact what they believe about themselves. She describes two general mindsets that she discovered in her research. These fixed and growth mindsets significantly impact a person's attitudes, behaviors, and personal success.[14]

A person with a fixed mindset thinks in terms of absolutes and believes that intelligence and ability are predetermined at birth. According to this thinking, people are born with special talents, and they cannot improve intelligence or ability over time with increased effort or persistence. These traits are innate or concrete and unchanging. If our intelligence and creative ability are static, then we are unable adapt or advance in meaningful ways. This leaves us striving for success and avoiding failure at all costs in an effort to look smart and evade looking foolish. This fixed mindset may prevent us from failure in the short-term because we focus only on those things we are good at accomplishing. However, over many years, it hampers our ability to learn new skills and impedes personal development.

Individuals with a growth mindset believe intelligence is dynamic, and it is possible to develop new skills and abilities through sustained effort and hard work. Achievements are not determined by special endowment of intellect, but rather can be attained by a drive for self-improvement. People with this mindset inherently believe that nearly everything about a person is moldable and can be changed. If we embrace this mindset, we are able to free ourselves from self-imposed limits and barriers. Personal growth and success are the outcome of our determination, hard work, and diligence. This growth mindset allows us to seek challenge and view mistakes and failure as opportunities to learn and grow.

As powerful as the growth mindset is for everyone, it is infinitely more important for the success of entrepreneurs. The average employee may be able to get away with the incremental thinking and failure avoidance associated with the fixed mindset. However, entrepreneurs would not likely even attempt to get started if they are paralyzed by the fear associated with the fixed mindset.

Nor would entrepreneurs take the risks necessary to break through in a market with formidable incumbent competitors or in an industry experiencing rapid technological change if they didn't believe success could be achieved through hard work and continuous learning. To ultimately win and achieve success in the long run, entrepreneurs must make a commitment to sustained, lifelong learning.

CHAPTER THREE

Planning the Journey

by Jim Stovall

Now that you have hopefully decided to dedicate your life to taking the journey of entrepreneurship, the question of a vehicle must be addressed. All entrepreneurs are unique. It is not a one-size-fits-all proposition. There are serial entrepreneurs who go from venture to venture mostly dependent upon the potential of the opportunity as opposed to the specific industry; there are specific entrepreneurs who may have expertise within a very narrow field and only become involved in entrepreneurial ventures within that arena. There are generational entrepreneurs like my friend and colleague, Steve Forbes, whose grandfather started the company, and then his father built it up before Steve Forbes took over the organization. Even though the Forbes organization has been functioning for decades, Steve Forbes, as an entrepreneur, put his mark on the enterprise and took it in new directions.

And then there are intrapreneurs who work somewhat as independent enterprises within a larger corporate umbrella. There are as many variations and permutations of entrepreneurship as there are individual entrepreneurs.

When it comes to selecting your own entrepreneurial vehicle to get you from where you are to where you want to be, the best advice I have ever heard is, "Find a need and fill it." Opportunities come disguised as problems, and big opportunities come disguised as big problems.

My own journey into entrepreneurship began with the biggest problem I have ever faced in my life. I clearly remember the morning I woke up and instantly realized that I had lost the remainder of my sight. My vision had been declining for over a decade, but eventually it dwindled away to nothing. I jumped out of bed that morning and staggered into the bathroom. I flipped on the light but still found myself in total darkness. I stared toward where I knew the mirror was hanging on the wall, but I could see nothing there at all.

It was a day I had been both dreading and expecting for years. The thoughts, doubts, and fears that came over me that morning would be impossible to describe to you. I was 29 years old, had never met a blind person, and I didn't have a clue what I was going to do with the rest of my life.

The only plan I could come up with that morning involved moving into a little 9-by-12-foot room in the back of our house. In my little room, I gathered my telephone, my radio, and my tape recorder and placed them near my chair in the corner. That corner of the room became my entire world. The thought of traveling millions of miles and speaking to millions of people in arena events, or running a television network with more than a thousand stations, or writing more than fifty books—having eight of them turned into movies— or any of the other activities I routinely perform today would have seemed as foreign to me then as going to the moon. I couldn't imagine ever getting out of my room, much less going anywhere or doing anything.

An Entrepreneurial Opportunity

I sat in my little 9-by-12-foot, self-imposed prison month after month getting more depressed and more discouraged each day. I would probably still be there today except for the fact that an entrepreneurial opportunity presented itself to me in the form of a monumental problem.

People around the world fervently pursue a great idea. They believe that if they could have that one vision or inspiration of a cutting edge concept that they could bring to the world, all their problems would be over and they could live the life of their dreams. Ironically, as these people are chasing ideas, they unknowingly and inadvertently trip over great ideas virtually on a daily basis. The only thing you have to do to have a great idea is to go through your daily routine, wait for something bad to happen, and ask yourself, "How could I have avoided that?" The answer to that question is a great idea.

The only thing you have to do to turn your great idea into a business is to ask yourself one further question, "How can I help other people avoid that?" The answer to that question is a great business opportunity. The world will give you fame, fortune, and everything you ever wanted as an entrepreneur if you will just focus on other people and solve their problems.

Oftentimes, people mistakenly believe that entrepreneurs are independent Lone Rangers who go their own way without any bosses or direction and do whatever they want. In reality, when you're an entrepreneur, everyone you serve as a customer, client, or prospect becomes your boss, and you can only succeed to the extent that you meet their needs, solve their problems, and keep them satisfied. As in many endeavors in life, in the world of entrepreneurship, it isn't about you, it's about those you serve.

Finding a Need and Fulfilling It

I have millions of books in print, and each of them—including the one you're reading right now—has my contact information in it. I hear from countless people, literally from around the world, and among the most frequently asked questions when readers contact me is, "How do I make a lot of money?" I constantly have to inform people that the only people who make money work at the national mint and print currency or make coins. The rest of us have to earn money, and the only way you can earn money honorably and consistently is to meet people at the point of their need and solve their problems.

More aspiring entrepreneurs seem to wrestle with the question of what kind of business they should start or pursue than any other question. I believe it's important to pursue your passion, particularly in an entrepreneurial startup venture. There are really virtually no good or bad businesses. There are simply businesses for which people have passion while others do not. You can find people all around the world becoming wildly successful bringing the most unlikely products and services to the marketplace. These people succeed because they have found a need and filled it with passion. The advent of global digital connectivity has opened the door for countless new opportunities; but at the same time, it has created a level of competition the world has never known.

When you look at competing in a crowded field, the best way I know to win is to pursue your passion. If you launch a venture simply because you read an article about it or somebody told you it was a good idea, you will likely pursue it as if you had a job and you were working for someone else. If you're competing against someone who is pursuing their passion and feels as if they are fulfilling their life's calling, you are unlikely to be able to sustain a level of high performance that will allow you to prevail in the marketplace.

Determining and Selecting Your Vehicle

Selecting your vehicle takes time and the hard work of introspection and self-evaluation. You must confront hard questions that are specific to you and will become fundamental to your business. What are you passionate about? What do you do better than anyone else? What tasks are easy for you that are hard for everyone else around you? And, what keeps you energized, focused, and awake at night?

Michael Jordan was arguably the greatest basketball player of all time. During the height of his career, he decided to pursue playing professional baseball. Even though Jordan was a world-class athlete and in incredible condition, his best efforts only resulted in him being a mediocre Minor League baseball player. If Michael Jordan had not found the right vehicle for his career, you and I would have never heard of him. The difference between being an unknown minor leaguer struggling in mediocrity and an iconic champion known around the world, is simply finding the right vehicle.

It's vital that you know what results you want to get out of entrepreneurship. What do you want to achieve? What lifestyle do you want to live? Picking the right vehicle is a matter of knowing where you want to go.

Where Do You Want to Go?

In the classic story, *Alice in Wonderland* by Lewis Carroll, Alice approaches a fork in the road where she meets a Cheshire cat. Alice asks the cat which road she should take. The cat inquired, "Where do you want to go?" Alice shrugged and responded, "I don't know." The cat offered Alice, as well as you and me, a great deal of wisdom stating, "If you don't know where you want to go, it really doesn't matter what road you take." When you consider entrepreneurship, if you don't know where you want to end up, it really doesn't matter which vehicle you select.

Early in my writing and speaking career, I had the privilege of working with Dr. Robert Schuller. We were discussing some ventures I was considering and with respect to one opportunity, I remember telling Dr. Schuller, "I don't know how to do that. I don't have any of the resources, and I don't have any contacts in that field." Dr. Schuller laughed and responded with that profound voice he used to dispense great amounts of wisdom, "Jim, don't ever get the question of how you are going to do something mixed up in the question of what you are going to do."

Dr. Schuller went on to explain to me that if we only pursue opportunities that are currently within our abilities, skill set, contacts, and resources, we will never grow beyond where we currently are. Instead, we should decide what it is we want to do, then burn the bridge, lock the door, and throw away the key. Once we have made the decision for what we are going to do, then we can address the question of how we are going to do it.

The Problem, The Idea

As I sat hopeless and helpless in the darkness of my 9-by-12-foot room, I was struck by the cruel irony of the fact that before I had lost my sight, that room had been our television room. I knew that a few feet away from me sat our television, video player, and my collection of classic movies. I've always been a fan of John Wayne, Cary Grant, Katharine Hepburn, and all of the stars of the golden age of the film industry. One day after sitting in my isolated room for several months, out of sheer boredom, I decided to play one of the classic movies.

Obviously I knew I wouldn't be able to see it, but I thought since I had watched most of the films so many times, I might be able to just listen to them and remember the plot as I heard the soundtrack. I selected an old Humphrey Bogart film entitled, *The Big Sleep*. In the classic story, Bogart plays the iconic character Philip Marlowe, a hard-boiled private detective.

It actually worked for a while, and I could sort of remember the movie; but then, as I listened, a shot was fired, someone screamed, a car sped away, and I forgot what happened. I got frustrated and said the magic words, "Somebody ought to do something about that."

The next time you think or say those words, you just had a great idea. The Narrative Television Network, which became the foundation for all my other entrepreneurial ventures, was conceived at that moment. It took many more difficult months before the venture was painfully born; and it took several more years of hard work before our company grew to adulthood, but it became a reality at that moment of frustration in my little 9-by 12-foot room in the back of my house.

I didn't know anything about producing, distributing, or presenting movies or television. I didn't know anything about it or what to do next, but I knew I had found my passion, and I was willing to stake my existence on making it a reality.

Among my more than fifty books, without a doubt, the most literary title I have ever written is my novel, *Keeper of the Flame.* It is an ethereal story of a mysterious figure that takes the reader on a guided tour of the most significant times and places in human history. Among the many stories in that particular book, is a parable I wrote about two groups of people who lived in ancient times. One group lived in the valley, tilled the soil, grew crops, and resided in a peaceful village along the banks of a gently flowing river. The other group of people were hunters and fierce warriors who lived among the mountain peaks that surrounded the river valley.

The two groups were suspicious of one another and avoided contact until the day when several of the hunter/warriors came down from the mountains and kidnapped the child of the chief of the village. The chief of the valley people called his strongest and most loyal soldiers together, and they pursued the kidnappers into the mountains. As they had never climbed mountains before and had no idea where they were going, their efforts eventually stalled out, and they knew they couldn't go any farther.

Just as they were turning to retreat down the mountain in utter defeat, one of the soldiers glanced up toward the mountain top and saw a lone figure descending toward them. As the figure approached, the chief realized it was his wife carrying their baby who had been kidnapped. As she joined the group, the chief and all of his soldiers were joyous and overwhelmed with emotion.

One of the soldiers asked the chief's wife, "How is it that you were able to climb the mountain and recover your child when the strongest and bravest soldiers in our village couldn't do it?"

The mother held her child and responded, "It wasn't your baby."

You and I must make sure that our entrepreneurial venture is our "baby." It is the project, concept, or product for which we are willing to go the extra mile and do whatever it takes to achieve success.

As I considered the possibility of the vehicle that has become Narrative Television Network, I discovered that movies and television are the number one recreational activity in our world today, and I discovered that there were 13 million blind and visually impaired people in the United States with many millions more around the world.

Additionally, I discovered that countless visually impaired children could go to school and be educated with their sighted peers if educational videos and school programming were simply made accessible for them. As I sat in the dark in our former TV room in the back of my house, I realized that I had discovered my baby and my entrepreneurial vehicle.

CHAPTER FOUR

Creative Capacity

by Dr. Kevin Schneider

Behind all brilliant ideas, every ground-breaking solution, and each wildly successful business is a creator. Unlike the discredited theory of spontaneous generation, ideas, solutions, and companies don't just spring into existence from nothing. They are thought into existence by a creator, an inventor, an entrepreneur.

Creativity is perhaps the fundamental common denominator of all entrepreneurs. It distinguishes the optimists who dream up possibilities from the pessimists who anticipate the worst to happen, and it separates the entrepreneurs who think up solutions to problems from the employees who look to others to solve their problems. Although some people may appear more inherently creative than others, it is a misconception to believe that only a handful of innovative geniuses are endowed with the gift of creativity.

David Burkus debunks the idea that only a rare breed of uniquely gifted individuals are creative in his book *The Myths of Creativity*. He explains how there are many myths about creativity we believe like the "Originality Myth" that suggests ideas are original only to their creators or the "Expert Myth" that implies solutions to difficult problems are best produced by experts. Another similar myth Burkus defines as the "Lone Creator Myth" describes the inclination to assign breakthrough discoveries to a single person. All of these myths share an underlying fallacy that ideas and their creators tend to exist in isolation, when in fact the opposite is true. Most ideas are not entirely original but are combinations of older ideas, solutions to intractable problems commonly require input from outsiders, and creativity is often a team effort.[1]

In their book *Creative Confidence*, Tom and David Kelley share the belief that we are all creative. Creativity is not confined to the lucky few, but rather everyone has far more creative potential than we can imagine. They believe that creative confidence is the assurance that you can change the world. Belief that you are creative is central to innovation, and this conviction provides us with the self-assurance that we can achieve our goals and aspirations.

And the Kelley brothers have the evidence to prove their theory. Through the Stanford d.school and IDEO, they have educated thousands of entrepreneurs and executives with mindsets and methods and helped innovative companies from large corporations to startups and social enterprises develop and market breakthrough ideas.[2]

In their efforts to teach people creativity, the Kelleys found that their students already had it in abundance. It was their job to help people discover their creative capacity through imparting new mindsets and developing new skills. They describe that tapping into your creative capacity is like discovering you have been driving with the emergency brake on, and then experiencing the ease of driving once it is released. Fortunately, we don't have to fabricate creativity from nothing. We do, however, often have to rediscover our creative potential. Once we revive this ability to dream and imagine again, we need the courage to act on those ideas.[3]

Born Creative

We are born with an incredible creative capacity. Anyone who has raised children can tell you that kids are wildly creative. At this current writing, I have two elementary-aged children. From hours spent drawing and painting to role playing to silly dance parties, their creative outlets are endless. And it seems that they have a question or get an idea about every four seconds. Whether they are inquiring about exploring other planets or get a brilliant idea about solving one of our everyday problems (that may work or end in disaster), they are constantly musing about an expanding list of topics. Their minds are sponges searching for the next moment of inspiration.

I remember being like this when I was young. I enjoyed drawing, making up stories, and playing every kind of make-believe game for hours. Then something happened as I grew older—I became a successful student. As a "smart" student in school, I learned to focus on the core subjects of math, English, and science. I discovered I had a fairly good photographic memory where I could visualize and remember obscure facts from my studies that I could regurgitate on exams.

I learned some other things as well. I realized I wasn't really very "good" at drawing, particularly compared to my classmates. My peers (mostly jocks) thought dancing was for girls, I of course shared this belief. The arts became more of a nuisance to me that held little value for acceptance into a university and ultimately securing a well-paying job.

The process of becoming less creative as I progressed through school is not unique to my personal story. Sir Ken Robinson, one of the world-renown experts on creativity, writes and speaks passionately about how our education system has had a detrimental effect on young, creative minds. Designed to support the industrial revolution, our modern education system focuses on generating productive workers rather than creative individuals. According to Robinson, "We don't grow into creativity; we grow out of it." In fact, "We are educating people out of their creativity," Robinson advocates.[4]

He believes we are born with magnificent natural capacities, but we can lose these intrinsic qualities as we are influenced by the world around us.[5] Perhaps this is why Tom and David Kelley describe how they help people rediscover their creativity. We were born with it, and if we lose it along the way for one reason or another, we must rediscover it.

This was certainly my experience. I remember the imaginative days of my youth, but as I grew older, I began to have negative experiences in classes relating to the arts. At one point, I had lost much of my creative freedom to the extent that I did not consider myself creative at all. I can clearly recall this period of time where I honestly believed that I was not a creative person.

For me personally, this lasted until a series of spiritual experiences occurred in my life when I met a transcendent God who revealed Himself to me as Creator. Through these deep, personal experiences, I discovered that I am made in the image of my Creator. These encounters had a profound, transformative effect on my mind that completely shifted the view of my creative capacity. I reasoned that if I am created in the image of a Creator, that I also have inherent creative qualities. This completely changed my perspective.

As I began to reflect on my middle and high school years, it occurred to me that I had narrowly equated drawing and painting with creativity. I realized that although I could not draw well compared to my peers, I could make up ridiculous stories. This realization led me to sign up for the speech and drama club at my school, and I found a creative outlet through improv.

Rediscover Your Creativity Capacity

There is a saying that "curiosity killed the cat." However, just the opposite is true in relation to inspiring creativity. If you want to rediscover your creative capacity, I suggest that "the absence of curiosity kills creativity." Like the enthusiastic creativity so commonly found in children, we must find a way to foster a sense of curiosity and imagination if we desire to be creative.

Curiosity is generally believed to be one of the driving forces behind exploration and the pursuit of knowledge. It provides the fuel, or passion, for learning. Curiosity is what compelled historic thinkers and creators like Leonardo da Vinci. Although most famously known for his paintings, da Vinci was not only a Renaissance artist, he was also an engineer and scientist. According to Michael Gelb, we all come into the world curious. This curiosità, as Gelb calls it, is an impulse or desire to learn more. He explains that da Vinci possessed an insatiable curiosità that "fueled the wellspring of his genius throughout his adult life."[6]

While curiosity involves seeking knowledge and experiences, creativity enables you to transform what you have learned and experienced into something unique and valuable. In other words, cultivating curiosity can be a seed for creativity.[7] Elon Musk is one of the most unique entrepreneurs of our era. As a serial entrepreneur, Musk is the entrepreneurial visionary behind billion-dollar companies in three different industries: automotive, renewable energy, and aerospace. This is no small feat. Tesla is disrupting the automotive industry through popularizing electric cars, SolarCity is harnessing solar energy to power homes and businesses across the country, and SpaceX has privatized space transportation.

In her research study on successful entrepreneurs, Amy Wilkinson describes that, "Curiosity supersedes credentials," and, "The creator's most important tool is curiosity." Curiosity is what drove Musk to move to the United States because he believes the country is "a nation of explorers." Musk was a voracious reader who consumed comic books and novels. He even read the encyclopedia from cover to cover. Revealing his wide-ranging interests, Musk asked dates, "What are the three things that will have the greatest impact on the future of humanity?"

He continued to exhibit a keen inquisitiveness as he made discoveries that led to founding companies in one industry after another, and Wilkinson suggests that making breakthrough discoveries and seizing opportunities ultimately has more to do with curiosity than talent, connections, or resources.[8]

If you think about it, boundless curiosity is the engine that drives creativity in children. My wife and I will forever remember the stage of development when our daughter was rapidly acquiring her language skills between the ages of one and two years old. We can never forget how she would point and ask, "What this is?" over and over throughout the day. She would continue to focus her inquiries on some specific object until she mastered the word. Just as quickly as she figured out the new concept, she was on to the next thing. These new objects would then appear in her stories and drawings. It is truly amazing how quickly inquisitive children learn, and nurturing curiosity can help us rediscover creativity at any age.

Accelerate Your Creative Potential

Whether you are in the process of rediscovering your creative capacity or are already confident of your creative abilities, how do we accelerate or maximize our creative potential? In his book *The Element: How Finding Your Passion Changes Everything,* Ken Robinson uses the concept of the element to describe the intersection between our passions and talents. Discovering what we are passionate about and what we are good at provides an environment where we can grow creatively.

Many famously creative people did not do well in school and were overlooked by others. These, of course, were incredibly gifted individuals, but their passions were not ignited and their talents were undiscovered in the environments in which they lived.[9]

For instance, Sir Paul McCartney, one of the most famous musicians of all time, made it through his entire education without anyone recognizing he had any real musical talent. McCartney loved music, but he found his music lessons at school uninteresting. He was even rejected by the Liverpool Cathedral when applying to join the choir. Imagine this, the Paul McCartney of the Beatles, turned down when attempting to join a local choir. The same was true of Elvis Presley and Mick Fleetwood.

Widely known as the "King of Rock and Roll," Elvis was prevented entrance into the local glee club because they believed his voice would ruin their sound. Fleetwood was a total failure in traditional academia, but he later found he had incredible passion and talent for playing the drums. McCartney, Presley, and Fleetwood were all initially deemed failures. However, once they found their passion and developed their musical talents, the rest is history.[10]

If you want to accelerate your creative potential through harnessing your passion and developing your talents, find your flow. Psychologist Mihaly Csikszentmihalyi defines flow as "the state in which people are so involved in an activity that nothing else seems to matter; the experience itself is so enjoyable that people will do it even at great cost, for the sheer sake of doing it."

Flow encompasses the positive aspects of human experience such as joy and creativity, and people find their flow through engaging in activities they enjoy.[11] Another way of putting it is that flow means to be "in the zone," which is a common phenomenon experienced by athletes when they are performing at the top of their game.

Research has demonstrated that flow can be a powerful catalyst for boosting creativity. In his book *Creativity: Flow and the Psychology of Discovery and Invention*, Csikszentmihalyi describes that, "Creative persons differ from one another in a variety of ways, but in one respect they are unanimous: They all love what they do. It is not the hope of achieving fame or making money that drives them; rather, it is the opportunity to do the work that they enjoy doing." Whether those interviewed were scientists, artists, or business professionals, the answer was the same: they enjoy what they do. And when people were asked to choose from a list that describes how they feel when they are doing what they enjoy most, they often chose "designing or discovering something new."[12]

If you want to experience flow, there are several important elements that we need to consider. For instance, there needs to be goals that clarify what needs to be done, and we need immediate feedback to our actions. There should be a balance between challenge and ability. If the task is too difficult, we can get agitated and frustrated. If it is too easy, we get bored. Finding flow requires uniting action and awareness while minimizing or eliminating distractions.

Like a basketball player attempting a game-winning free throw, we must be able to completely concentrate on what we are doing in the moment. Finding flow also means that we lose consciousness of self and we do not fear failure. We must simply be too focused on what we are doing to be concerned about safeguarding our ego. Ultimately, when we are in a state of flow, we lose track of time, and the activity becomes an end in itself.[13]

Because creativity involves generating novel ideas and solutions, the act of discovery in the creative process tends to be one of the most enjoyable activities in which a person can be engaged. The inverse is also true. When we enjoy what we do, we tend to be more creative. Successful entrepreneurs and innovative companies understand this connection between creativity and fun. According to Richard Branson, "A business has to be evolving, it has to be fun, and it has to exercise your creative interests."

Google is famous for the extent to which it has focused on promoting a fun culture of creativity. From free food to pool and ping pong tables to allowing pets at work, Google prides itself on producing happy, motivated employees. Therefore, we can learn from research studies as well as examples from well-known entrepreneurs and innovative companies that it is possible to accelerate our creative potential by discovering what we are passionate about, developing our talents, finding our flow, and enjoying what we do.

CHAPTER FIVE

Preparing for the Journey

by Jim Stovall

You've heard it said that "the journey of a thousand miles begins with one step." This may be true, but your entrepreneurial journey must begin with a number of steps. Now that you've decided to be an entrepreneur and are selecting your vehicle, it's critical to get ready for the trip.

Entrepreneurs are often free spirits and want to fly by the seat of their pants leaving everything up in the air and simply planning to deal with it later. Nothing will destroy your dreams and your entrepreneurial journey faster than failing to prepare for the contingencies and putting the proper people in proper places. It's not a matter of if challenges and problems will arise, it's a matter of when they will arise. Dealing with contingencies in advance can spell the difference between a minor bump in the road and a total journey-ending crash and burn.

The first thing you need to prepare for your upcoming journey is your attitude. Even though I had conceived of my entrepreneurial vehicle, I was still stuck in my 9-by-12-foot room. Before I could change the world, I had to change my own mindset and get out of my mental prison. Then, within a few days, two different individuals entered my space and competed for dominance in my mind.

The first individual was a state government worker who dealt with people with disabilities. He showed up at my home and came into my 9-by-12-foot room with a white cane and a very limited plan for the rest of my life. I told him I wanted to start a business, help other people like me, and become successful. He laughed out loud, set the white cane beside my chair, and explained, "You need to come to terms with your new reality. You're never going to go anywhere or do anything, and you will never be more than a few feet from this white cane." He went on to explain my potential existence within a sheltered workshop or facility for profoundly disabled people.

At about that same time, another individual came into my room in the form of an audiotape given to me by a friend and neighbor. I put the tape into my player and heard the uplifting voice of Dr. Denis Waitley. Dr. Waitley has since become a dear friend and mentor of mine, he wrote the Foreword to my first book, and we have shared the stage on many occasions. But on that particular day via the cassette tape I had been given, he recited his epic poem, "If You Think You Can, You Can."

So as I sat in the darkness of my 9-by-12-foot room, which made up my entire world, on one side of my chair, I had a white cane that represented limitation, hopelessness, and despair. On the other side of my chair, a voice filled with possibility, certainty, and success emanated from my tape player. The beginning of my climb from that pit of despair came when I thought of the two individuals and what they stood for. I remember voicing my thoughts out loud, "Somebody is lying to me."

Hope and Possibility

I chose to give hope and possibility a chance, and that decision has made all the difference. The first day I emerged from my 9-by-12-foot room, I didn't win an Emmy Award, write a best-selling book, or make a million dollars. I walked 52 feet down my driveway to my mailbox. It was one of the hardest things I have ever done. I was shaking like a leaf and drenched in sweat as I reached out my hand and touched the mailbox, which was my destination for my first journey out of my room.

As I stood there with my hand on the mailbox, my foot touched the curb at the edge of my street. Even though I had lived in that house for over a decade as a sighted person, I discovered something that day I had never known before. I realized, for the first time, that I lived on a miraculous street. I understood that my street led to the corner, and connected with another street, which intersected with another street, which would eventually take me anywhere in the world I wanted to go. This was an amazing revelation for someone who had been stuck in an 9-by-12-foot room.

Success comes from certainty, and certainty comes from possibility that grows out of hope. My entrepreneurial venture and eventual success was a million miles away, but for the first time I had hope and a road on which to begin my journey.

After finally emerging from my 9-by-12-foot room, I slowly ventured back into the real world. One of my first outings was to attend a support group for blind people. I was in hope that I could learn more about the physical, mental, and emotional aspects of living without sight. It is critical in life and in entrepreneurship to seek advice and expertise whenever possible. However, you should never take advice from anybody who hasn't been where you want to be or done what you want to do. There are a myriad of fakes and frauds in the field of entrepreneurship who will take your money and waste your time if you're not careful.

When I wrote the book, *The Millionaire Map*, which recounts my own journey from poverty to prosperity, I first dictated those words, "Don't take advice from anyone who doesn't have what you want." When those words were read back to me as we reviewed the manuscript, I realized I would have to do something very uncomfortable. I talked to Crystal and the rest of my family and made the decision to print a statement from Merrill Lynch and Bank of America regarding my net worth within the pages of that book. As you read this book, if you want to confirm that I have been where you want to go, you might check out *The Millionaire Map*. It describes that—excluding the value of my companies, real estate, and book and movie royalties—my savings and investment portfolio has in excess of $10 million. That book was written several years ago, and I'm pleased to report that the numbers have continued to grow.

In our society, we have taboos against talking about politics, sex, religion, and money. I'm a firm believer that everyone's personal finances are their personal business until they ask me to invest some of my time, effort, or energy in their advice or counsel. At that point, their business becomes my business. Advice from fat diet doctors, imprisoned lawyers, or broke entrepreneurs should be avoided.

Hello, My Name Is

I was nervous and uncomfortable as I settled into my chair at the support group for blind people. I was not comfortable being out in public, and the whole topic of blindness was difficult and depressing to me at that time. As I was waiting for the meeting to start, I heard someone approach me, and the person said, "Hello, my name's Kathy Harper." I introduced myself and we began to talk.

Kathy was a legally blind, single mom who worked for one of the best law firms in our part of the country. She had partial sight and could still do her computer work at the law firm. However, her long-term prognosis was not good. In the course of our conversation, I shared with her my frustrating experience with the Humphrey Bogart movie. I had given it a lot of thought, and I told Kathy, "If someone would just add the voice of a narrator between the existing dialogue within a movie, TV show, or educational program, it would become accessible to millions of people like you and me." Without hesitation, Kathy responded, "When are we going to do that?"

I was in shock as I thought that it was all I could do to get to this meeting. The idea of starting a new entrepreneurial venture seemed beyond impossible. Finally, Kathy followed up on the question that I had not answered saying, "Oh, I thought you were serious. I didn't realize you were just talking." Whether she realized it or not, she somehow tapped into the last vestige of my competitive spirit from when I was an athlete, and at that moment, the Narrative Television Network (NTN) was born.

NTN became the foundation for all of our other related enterprises. It is my passion, my vocation, and my avocation. Today, through our foundation, we support many charities and nonprofit organizations, but few of them do as much true good in the world as Narrative

Television Network. Kathy became a great friend, a treasured colleague, and the perfect traveling companion for this entrepreneurial journey.

I have long believed, as the great author, speaker, and thought-leader Jim Rohn said, "We become like the five people we hang around with most." When we understand that our success, our attitudes, our mindset, and our income will grow out of the influences of the people with whom we spend the most time, it becomes vital to purposefully consider who we are going to spend time with. I believe we should all create our entrepreneurial dream team. Think of your entrepreneurial venture and make a list of the people you would most want to advise, influence, and mentor you.

A Dream Team

When Kathy and I began the Narrative Television Network, it was a totally unique concept. The idea of making the visual world accessible to a blind person is as old as the first blind cave man with a friend describing the world to him. We later discovered that other people had made efforts in making media accessible. As Kathy and I sat down at her dining room table to discuss our new venture, we didn't know anything about television distribution, programming, or any other elements of the industry. When we started the list of prospects to become a part of our dream team, the first name that came to mind was Ted Turner.

Mr. Turner had forged so many new concepts in the television and media industry. At a time when TV news consisted of a thirty-minute daily broadcast, he conceived of and launched CNN. He took a fledgling UHF station in Atlanta and turned it into the super-station TBS. He bought the MGM classic film library and created a 24-hour TV network featuring classic movies, as well as many other groundbreaking innovations within the industry.

I wrote a one-page letter to Mr. Turner in Atlanta telling him who I was and what I was going to do. As improbable as it may seem, from that meager effort, Ted Turner became an advisor and a friend for the next thirty years and remains so at this writing. Countless times being able to call on his wisdom and experience or simply having his name associated with our company made all the difference.

When we expanded into writing and speaking within the financial realm, Steve Forbes headed the wish list for my dream team, and I'm grateful that he remains a friend and advisor to this day. He has endorsed several of my books and written the Foreword to others. We have spoken at events together, and he actually played himself in a small cameo role in our movie, *The Lamp*, based on my novel.

When I initially became an author and thought about who I would most want to have on my writing dream team, the name Mark Victor Hansen came to mind. Mark is the co-author of the *Chicken Soup for the Soul* series and among the bestselling authors alive today. When I asked him to endorse my first novel, *The Ultimate Gift*, Mark wrote these words for the book cover, "I love this book. I see this book becoming one of the great and inspiring movies of all time. It touches my heart and soul deeply, profoundly, and permanently, and will yours too. Happy reading of *The Ultimate Gift*." I believe Mark's words on that book cover launched us into the movie business, which has now become a multimillion-dollar part of our entrepreneurial venture.

Right People, Places, Time, Reasons

In addition to your dream team, you must surround yourself with a group of professionals dedicated to getting you from where you are to where you want to be. As you form your organization, you will want to have the best legal and accounting talent you can find. Many entrepreneurs find themselves out of business and in debt due to legal and accounting problems that could have been avoided with a bit of planning.

When you grow to the point where you are hiring employees, it is critical that you get the right people in the right places at the right time and for the right reasons. No one succeeds on their own. I am more aware of this than most people because, as a blind person, I can't even get to my office in the morning without the assistance of one of my team members. When you dedicate your professional life to creating TV for the blind, write books you can't read, and make movies you can't watch, you remain ever mindful of the value and necessity of a great team.

As an entrepreneur, you are going to spend an inordinate amount of time working on your venture. Since entrepreneurship allows you to be the boss, you may as well select people you respect, like, and with whom you enjoy spending time. It's important that the people on your team are not only good for you, but that you are also good for them.

I have had people on our team who were aspiring singers and songwriters who now have performed music in major movies we produced. I've had team members who use their voice in local radio who were able to join our team and use their talent to help blind people around the world enjoy movies and TV. My talented colleague, Beth Sharp, who is typing these words as I dictate, has a passion for training dogs so they can be adopted into loving families. Her beloved dog, Cooper, appeared with Academy Award-winner Louis Gossett Jr. in one of our movies. Having a great team around you is a two-way street.

Support and Accountability

In addition to your dream team and employees, you need to be part of entrepreneurial support and accountability groups. I have been in an accountability group for more than twenty-five years with people who know me, care about me, and hold me accountable. They understand entrepreneurship and know the unique challenges I face. In your entrepreneurial journey, you will have doubts, fears, and times you just need to talk to someone who understands what you're going through.

You will face many distractions, diversions, and opportunities to get off track as you launch your entrepreneurial venture. When you are bogged down in frustration trying to birth your dream into reality, there will be times when the grass seems greener elsewhere, and you will be tempted to take a detour from your journey. This should be avoided and should be thoroughly discussed with your dream team, accountability group, and your entrepreneurial support team.

Today we have many facets to our entrepreneurship, but it's important to realize that it all began with the Narrative Television Network. The success of NTN gave me opportunities to speak at industry meetings and conventions. That success opened the door for me to become a highly compensated professional speaker. Success on the platform opened the world of authorship to me and, to date, as mentioned previously, eight of my books have been turned into movies. I also write a weekly syndicated column that appears in newspapers, magazines, and online publications around the world, and I do both a local and a national radio show each week.

Synergy

At first glance, it might appear that our efforts are scattered across the entrepreneurial landscape. However, we are in the message business, and we create intellectual property. When you understand this, you will see the synergy among our five business groups. I always visualize this as a four-sided pyramid with a point on the top. Whatever activity we are pursuing at any giving moment in time is the point. The point must be supported by and support each of the four sides of our pyramid.

For example, if I am writing a novel, we will pursue having that novel made into a movie. The movie, of course, will then be narrated for our core visually impaired audience, and we will promote both the book and the movie in my column, on the radio, and in my speeches. In this way, all of our efforts support one another.

I invest in other businesses outside my role as an entrepreneur. I own an energy company, a golf course, and a computer firm, among other outside interests; but if I'm going to be spending my time, effort, and energy, or that of our team, it must fit our pyramid and further our mission and our message.

The Blind Leading the Blind

You have never met anyone less qualified to do what they do or less likely to succeed than I was. As I left the support group for blind people that day, I had a vague dream in my mind and one partially sighted colleague willing to undertake this journey with me. We didn't know anything about where we were going or how to get there. I was blind, broke, and scared. My only guide to the sighted world was a legally blind, single mom willing to risk her career on me. I always treasured her loyalty and never questioned her wisdom.

As Kathy and I began our journey, we were figuratively and literally the blind leading the blind, but less than three years later, at an event in New York, the National Academy of Television Arts and Sciences presented us with an Emmy Award, and—just four short years after that—in a ceremony at our nation's capital, the President's Committee on Equal Opportunity named me Entrepreneur of the Year. Dreams do come true and your own dreams can become reality as part of your entrepreneurial journey.

CHAPTER SIX

Bet Your Beta

by Dr. Kevin Schneider

In 2017, Alex Honnold became the first person to free solo climb El Capitan in Yosemite National Park, California. El Capitan is an iconic peak that boasts sheer granite cliffs that rise 3,000 feet from the valley floor of Yosemite. Heralded as one of the greatest athletic achievements ever, Honnold climbed the vertical rock face with no ropes or assistance at all. The death-defying ascent shocked the rock climbing world due to the impossibility of the climb, and one slip could have caused Honnold to plunge to his death. Yet, Honnold was determined to attempt the legendary climb.

In a similarly daring feat, 16-year-old Abby Sunderland attempted to become the youngest person to sail solo around the world. Sunderland comes from a family of sailors, and she had been sailing since she was young. During her audacious voyage, she made it past the halfway mark, but then faced some technical challenges that slowed her progress. Stormy seas touting 50-foot waves in the Southern Indian Ocean later caused her to abandon her vessel due to a broken mast. This put her in real danger adrift in the middle of a raging ocean.

However, as a result of a coordinated effort involving US, Australian, and French rescue workers, Sunderland was eventually rescued by a French fishing vessel in a remote part of the Indian Ocean after she set off her emergency beacons.

I love sharing these stories partly because they are incredible and partly because of the reactions I often get from people. Sometimes the response is simply, "That is crazy! I would never do that." Dido. Other times, in the case of the 16-year-old sailor, listeners will criticize the parents who were so careless as to allow a young girl to do something so dangerous.

In fact, Sutherland's parents were heavily criticized by several reporters. Laurence Sunderland, the girl's father, provides an interesting insight in response to the criticism. He cited his daughter's competence—not her age or gender—as the determining factor in allowing her to attempt the daring exploit. He told the Associated Press, "Sailing and life in general is dangerous. Teenagers drive cars. Does that mean teenagers shouldn't drive a car? I think people who hold that opinion have lost their zeal for life. They're living in a cotton-wool tunnel to make everything safe."

These stories suggest that particular risks, even ones that may result in death, are not inherently the same for every person. Or in other words, there are factors that impact the relative riskiness of our actions, and we can take steps to reduce risks we may face when pursuing our dreams.

For instance, in Honnold's case, he had been studying El Capitan for years and believed it was doable to free-climb the peak. He practiced climbing El Capitan dozens of times with a rope before attempting the free-climb. From careful and consistent practice, Honnold had nearly memorized every square inch of the mountain.

Sunderland had become an expert sailor by the time she made her endeavored to circumnavigate the globe on her sailboat, and it was her dream to complete the solo trip around the world in her sailboat. Not only was she an expert sailor, but she had all the necessary equipment that prepared her for worst-case scenarios. She had even learned from her older brother who had successfully sailed around the world at age 17.

Although free-climbing and sailing each requires unique skill sets and have different risk profiles, Honnold and Sunderland's stories share very similar characteristics. Both Honnold and Sunderland dreamed, or even obsessed, over the goal they had in mind. They each had developed significant expertise in their respective fields; they had developed intimate knowledge of the risks involved; and they had studied, practiced, and envisioned achieving their impossible dreams.

Free-climbing and sailing around the world may be comparably riskier than many other physical activities, but Honnold and Sunderland were not ignorant of the risks. They understood the dangers involved, and through dedicated training and careful preparation, took meticulous steps to manage the risks to a level where they were confident to take the leap.

Discover Your Beta

What is your risk appetite? You might not dream of exceling at some impossible or dangerous sport or attempting an impossible athletic feat, but we do all take risks. As Sunderland's father suggested, we take a risk every time we get behind the wheel of a car. The trick then is comparing the riskiness of a particular activity relative to some standard measure. This will help us not only understand our personal perception of a particular risk, but it will also provide us with a way to more objectively assess or evaluate the risk against a specific standard. The concept of beta in the financial world is one way to think about how we approach risk.

One common definition of beta is understood in economic terms. It is used to measure the volatility, or riskiness, of a publicly traded stock. Beta provides a way to measure the financial return of a stock relative to the broader market. The general stock market such as the S&P 500 has a beta of 1.0, and the riskiness of individual stocks are measured against this standard. For example, let's suppose a stock has a beta of 1.5. If the broader market increases by 10 percent, then the stock would be expected to increase by 15 percent. The same goes if the general stock market declines. A stock with a beta greater than 1.0 would be expected to decrease by a greater amount based upon the size of its beta.

If we want to define risk, we should not only consider the dictionary definition that is merely limited to exposure to some sort of danger or loss. Rather, we need to understand that risk involves both the potential for loss as well as expectation of rewards.

Warren Buffett is the founder of Berkshire Hathaway and known as the most successful investor of all time. Buffett's portfolio has included iconic companies such as Bank of America, Coca-Cola, and Kraft Heinz. Investing in publicly traded stocks is risky—it has the potential for total financial loss as well as significant financial reward.

Buffett is famous for saying that he wouldn't invest in something he doesn't understand, which is why he had once said he didn't invest in tech stocks. Although Buffett has since taken financial positions in tech stocks, the underlying principle remains the same. He invests in companies with underlying business models that he understands.

It should come as no surprise that entrepreneurs typically have skills or expertise that relate to the particular dream or vision they have for starting a company. This combination of skill and ability with passion and desire can greatly diminish the inherent risk associated with a venture.

Take Sam Walton, for example. Walton did not launch Walmart without first gaining retail experience and developing an expertise in merchandising. After graduating from the University of Missouri, Walton joined a J.C. Penney management training program. He later opened his own Ben Franklin five-and-dime store. Over a number of years, he eventually operated a regional chain of Ben Franklin stores. It wasn't until company executives rejected Walton's idea for a new discount chain of retail stores targeting small Midwest towns that he opened his first Walmart store in Arkansas.

Therefore, to overcome the myriad of challenges associated with starting a business, it is essential that entrepreneurs discover and understand their beta, or risk profile. During a short stint as a financial advisor, I was accustomed to asking clients questions that would build their risk profile. If clients were overly risk averse, they should not allocate the majority of their money in equity markets. Investing a larger portion of their portfolio in bonds or fixed investments is more suitable for the risk-averse investor.

However, for those clients with a more significant appetite for risk, investing in tech stocks or international companies is more appropriate. The principles are the same for entrepreneurs. When launching a startup, entrepreneurs should understand their beta, and they can often reduce the inherent riskiness of the venture if they have developed relevant skills and expertise. In other words, entrepreneurs may be able to increase their potential for business success by making bets that are aligned with their individual skills and personal beta.

The Danger of Playing it Safe

Whether or not you have developed some level of experience or skill in a particular area, stepping out to launch a new venture can still be daunting. Uncertainty or fear can often cause us to stay in our comfort zone instead of taking the entrepreneurial leap. It may seem prudent to avoid risk by staying in our comfort zone.

However, have you ever thought to ask yourself what you may be giving up by playing it safe? To highlight this point, I will use another example including financial investments. As mentioned earlier, certain investments like publicly traded equities are riskier (or have a greater volatility) than other investments such as bonds. In other words, there is a greater potential for financial loss and gain.

When planning for retirement, it is common to estimate the future balance of investments needed to provide a certain level of monthly income. Then based upon a combination of factors, you can determine the amount of annual investment and rate of return needed to meet your financial goals. Let's consider the following set of assumptions. First, let's assume that I am 25 years old and believe that I need $1 million to retire in forty years. Let's also assume that the historic average rate of return of return of bonds is 5 percent and stocks is 8 percent. To retire at age 65, I would need to invest around $3,000 per year in stocks that provide an 8 percent return to meet my goal. However, I would need to invest approximately $8,000 per year in bonds that yield 5 percent per year.

Given the fact that bonds have a historically lower rate of return compared to stocks, you would need to invest a much larger amount of money over your life-time to meet your retirement goals. In reality, most young investors would never meet their financial goals if they were to invest in only bonds at a lower compara-tive rate of return. This example highlights the dangers of playing it safe in regard to investing.

For risk-averse investors, the thought that equities have a greater downside compared to bonds may deter them from investing in stocks. However, if they do not consider the potential upside associated with invest-ing in equities, then they may not realize what they are giving up in potential gains.

Playing it safe can also mean that we hesitate to accept new challenges, refrain from seeking to learn new skills, or avoid opportunities to gain new experiences. For many would-be entrepreneurs, this may result in never taking the leap to launch out on their own. Staying in our comfort zone may be the one thing preventing us from creating a great product or launching an innovative startup.

In an interview with Y Combinator, a company that invests seed money for startups, Facebook co-founder Mark Zuckerberg said that the best advice PayPal co-founder Peter Thiel ever gave him was, "In a world that's changing so quickly, the biggest risk you can take is not taking any risk." From the perspective of the self-made billionaire, playing it safe may be the riskiest thing that we can do.[1]

If playing it safe can be dangerous, then why is it sometimes so difficult to break out of our comfort zone to take entrepreneurial risks? Doug Sundheim, executive coach, consultant, and author, provides some helpful insights concerning why it is all too easy to play it safe. In his book *Taking Smart Risks: How Sharp Leaders Win When Stakes Are High,* he describes how we are keenly aware of the consequences of taking too much risk because the news media reminds us of these stories every day. Sundheim recounts, "Businesses, families, and individuals are ruined in shocking fashion–'150-year-old bank and pillar of Wall Street is gone in the blink of an eye'; 'Major oil company loses $90 billion in market value in three months'; 'Kite surfer tries his luck in a hurricane and slams into a building.' These common stories are an ever-present reminder of the dangers of taking risks."[2]

Sundheim continues to explain that we unfortunately don't hear the same messages about playing it safe because the dangers of staying in our comfort zone do not typically result in some sudden or dramatic disaster. The consequences of playing it safe don't make news headlines. For example, he suggests you will never see headlines that warn, "Low-risk approach forces local business to file for bankruptcy," or "Man retires after mediocre career and feels painful remorse for never having laid anything on the line." The real dangers of playing are much more subtle, overlooked, and uneventful. They develop gradually over a span of months and years and can be difficult or impossible to identify.

In fact, Sundheim suggests that the consequences of playing it safe can actually be more dangerous than measured risk-taking because, "…like a slow leak in a tire, you don't see or feel these dangers on a daily basis."[3]

Playing it safe may not only be potentially more threatening to our future success than taking risks, but it also frequently results in living a lackluster life according to author Neale Donald Walsch. Walsch believes, "Life begins at the end of your comfort zone." Have you ever felt stuck or bored in your career or life in general? Perhaps you are not taking enough risks. If you ask people when they have felt most alive, many times the answer will relate to some time in their life when they were taking risks.

One of the most exciting times in my educational career was during my doctoral research. I know what you are thinking—doctoral research has nothing to do with taking risks and is one of the most utterly boring activities on earth. Well, okay I agree, but I was not engaged in your average doctoral research study. I was conducting field research in rural villages in Afghanistan, and the results of my efforts had the potential to impact the lives of thousands of people. Although my research was extremely dangerous, the potential outcome of my work was worth the risk. In fact, as I look back, it was one of the times during the course of my life and career that I have felt the most alive.

Framing and Focus

In 1981, psychology researchers Amos Tversky and Daniel Kahneman discovered some interesting principles surrounding decision-making and risk by framing the same scenario in different ways. Their research uncovered what we now know as loss aversion bias. In other words, we are hardwired to avoid loss. The researchers made the discovery while conducting a study among university students.

Participants were asked to imagine the US is preparing for a disease outbreak expected to kill 600 people, and they must select one of two alternative programs illustrated in problems 1 and 2. Problem 1 describes the situation as follows. If Program A is accepted, 200 people will be saved. However, if Program B is adopted, there is a 1/3 chance 600 people will be saved and 2/3 chance no people will be saved.[4]

A second group of students were given a different framing of the same problem with separate programs labeled Program C and Program D. In the second problem, participants were told that 400 people would die if Program C was adopted. Alternatively, if Program D was adopted, there is a 1/3 chance no one would die, and 2/3 chance that 600 people would die. Although Programs A and C yielded exactly the same outcomes, 72 percent of respondents chose Program A while only 22 percent selected Program C.

Similarly, while Programs B and D were described as producing the same clinical results, only 28 percent of respondents selected Program B while 78 percent chose Program D. If the only difference between Programs A and C and Programs B and D was how the outcome was presented, then why did respondents' perception of risk change so drastically when the scenarios were presented differently?[5]

The divergence in results of the study have to do with framing and the perception of risk. Problem 1 focused on the potential number of lives that could be saved while problem 2 focused on the probability of lives that would be lost. Thus, the research study reveals that when people make decisions regarding gains, or rewards, they tend to be more risk averse.

Conversely, when people make choices involving loss, they often opt to take risks. The application for understanding how entrepreneurs may, or may not, take risks is important. We learn from this study that where we focus our attention—on what we may lose versus what we may gain—makes a big difference. In fact, Sundheim suggests, "Where we choose to focus our attention matters—big time. If we focus on something that we already possess, we probably won't take the risk. However, if we focus on what we might lose by not taking the risk, then we are more likely to take the risk." Either way we are acting with the risk-averse bias; it just matters what we choose to focus on.[6]

Little Bets and Small Wins

There is a myth that when it is time for eagles to learn to fly, their parents literally push them out of the nest. As they hurtle toward the ground, the story goes that the parent will swoop under the eaglet just before it falls to its death until the eagle can fly on its own. While this makes for an exhilarating story, adult eagles simply do not subject their young to such perilous risks. On the contrary, adult eagles allow the small eaglets to take much smaller risks as they learn to fly. Parents bring food directly to the eaglets after they are born, and they eventually begin to stretch their wings and jump around the nest as they get older.

Although the parents do not push the eaglets out of the nest, they do make efforts to coax the young birds. Instead of bringing food back to the nest as the young birds age, the adult eagles land on nearby branches so that the eaglets have to take short flights to retrieve the food. The adults use hunger, rather than death-defying fear, to encourage their young to make smaller bets gradually over time until the eaglets can soar through the air like their parents.

There is a similar misconception that entrepreneurs must take huge risks to be successful. While stories of famous entrepreneurs who took daring risks to build billion-dollar companies make riveting news headlines, it is simply not true that taking big risks is the only way—or even the most common way—to become a successful entrepreneur. In the book *Little Bets: How Breakthrough Ideas Emerge from Small Discoveries*, Peter Sims describes how entrepreneurs can make little bets to achieve great outcomes. Instead of taking a larger, winner-takes-all sized bet, Sims advocates taking smaller actions to discover and develop ideas that are both achievable and affordable. Because no one can see the future, little bets enable entrepreneurs to test ideas and refine solutions.

For instance, when Howard Schultz launched the coffee shop concept in the US, it was originally modeled after Italian coffee houses where baristas wore bow ties and opera music played in the background. The idea eventually required many incremental iterations before Schultz had a winning concept that took off in the US market.[7]

Sims found that experimental innovators like Schultz come from a variety of industries and that several methods, rather than a formulaic model, form the basis for understanding how to make little bets. Experimentation, central to the little bets approach, also propelled Hewlett Packard as a market leader in the burgeoning technology industry during the latter part of the twentieth century. In one case, instead of making a large bet on launching a pricey new calculator, Hewlett decided to make a more affordable bet and only produce a thousand products to initially test the market before planning for mass production. The company scaled production only after the concept took off.

Sims found successful entrepreneurs who follow this approach immerse themselves in the context of the situation or problems facing customers while carefully gathering insights along the way. Ultimately, making small bets requires flexibility, pivots, and constant iteration when developing ideas and designing prototypes.[8]

The phenomenon of making little bets is similar to the theory of broken windows coined by social scientists James Wilson and George Kelling. According to this theory, seemingly small or insignificant signs of disorder such as a broken window lead to additional broken windows and greater disorder. This causes a snowball effect that eventually leads to increased vandalism and crime in neighborhoods.

For example, instead of initially targeting violent crimes such as muggings and homicides when cleaning up New York City in the 1980s and 1990s, Kelling focused on winning the battle against graffiti and farebeating in the subway system. David Gunn, hired as the new subway director, stated that, "Graffiti was symbolic of the collapse of the subway system." Similarly, William Bratton, head of the transit police, believed farebeating was the underlying sign of disorder in the subway system that led to more serious crimes. In tackling these problems—which seemed insignificant compared to more serious crime—both men initially focused on making little bets over many years to transform New York City.[9]

The result of little bets can also be viewed through the lens of achieving what organizational theorist Karl Weick refers to as small wins. According to Weick, a small win is "a concrete, complete, implemented outcome of moderate importance." Small wins often appear insignificant on their own, but a series of wins targeting small but important goals can develop patterns that produce noticeable results. Securing early success through this approach can set in motion forces that lead to opportunities for additional small wins. As a result of a series of small wins, resources often flow to winners which can enable them to eventually pursue larger wins.[10]

For entrepreneurs, this often requires prototyping concepts or developing a minimum viable product before investing significant resources into an idea. It may also mean setting realistic and adaptable milestones in an effort to attaining a much larger vision. And any entrepreneur will tell you that notching small wins creates momentum that is crucial in the early stages of a startup.

CHAPTER SEVEN

Beginning the Journey

by Jim Stovall

More aspiring entrepreneurs fail to start than all of the entrepreneurs who begin a venture and don't succeed. There is never a perfect time to begin. Procrastination will kill your dreams. It's easy to sit at home and wait for all the lights to turn green before you back out of the driveway. If you look at all of the multimillion- and multibillion-dollar entrepreneur success stories around the world, they each have one thing in common—they got started regardless of obstacles, barriers, or red lights. If you begin, I cannot guarantee you'll succeed; but if you don't start, I can guarantee you will fail.

Two of the most valuable traits an entrepreneur can have are the ability to pull the trigger and the ability pull the plug. These are decisions that should be made and established in advance. Pulling the trigger is simply a matter of pre-deciding when to start, move, or act. The more you can put all of your critical decisions on autopilot, the more successful you will be. Instead of evaluating and performing due diligence on every element of your venture, it's far better to determine exactly what you're looking for so that when you encounter it, you simply pull the trigger and move forward.

Pulling the plug is the process of pre-determining when you should deploy an exit strategy and live to fight another day. In all of my business ventures, I utilize a concept I call "accelerating your point of failure." The only thing worse than failing today is failing a year from now. The sooner you can get to the critical point, the sooner you can succeed with your current venture or build a better one. Engineers utilize this concept with mechanical devices as they stress each part of a machine to its breaking point. Great investors have a pre-determined buy and sell point so that they don't get caught up in the emotion of the moment.

As a former athlete, I can assure you that the best training regimens are established in advance. You don't wait until you're nearing the point of exhaustion to determine how far you want to go. The great NFL coach for whom the Superbowl trophy is named, Vince Lombardi, said, "Fatigue makes cowards of us all."

Imagination and Implementation

You must divide your entrepreneurial efforts into two arenas. You have the imagination component, and you have the implementation component. When you're imagining the possibilities for your venture, everything is possible, flexible, and creative; but when you begin to implement, you must plan your work and work your plan. If you adjust your plan in midstream, you will accept less than your best effort and your entrepreneurial venture will not live up to its potential.

My late, great friend and mentor, the legendary Coach John Wooden, was arguably the greatest coach of all time, winning ten NCAA basketball championships in twelve years. This is a feat that will likely never be repeated, and many sports experts believe it to be the greatest record of all time. Coach Wooden planned his practices meticulously. Every activity was written out and timed to the second. In this way, he could let his players know exactly what would be expected of them so they could implement the plan utilizing their greatest effort. On game days, Coach wooden generally sat on the bench and calmly enjoyed watching his players implement the plan. He knew that victories were won in the planning and practice stage.

Your business will succeed and fail based on your ability to implement your plan. If you don't have a business plan, you have a hobby. Business plans are not perfect and rarely mirror reality, but they give you a place to start and a track to run on as you implement. In entrepreneurship, when it's all said and done, there's a lot more said than done. You don't succeed based on your dreams, goals, or plans—even though they are critical. You succeed based on your implementation.

A Plan of Action

When we began the Narrative Television Network, I knew that I would have to get advertisers to support our programming. I had no idea how to do this, but I knew we needed a plan of action, and I would have to implement it. Kathy got out her big magnifying glass, which enabled her to read standard print, and we headed off—blind leading the blind—to our public library.

While there, she found a resource book that listed the top 100 advertisers in the US. That became my roadmap as well as my prospect list. I began calling them all each day. I've had people challenge me on this, arguing, "You can't call all one hundred advertisers every day." I assure you it can be done because I did it for months. It takes approximately six-and-a-half hours each day. When you're an unknown entrepreneur trying to sell advertising for a startup network for the blind, and you're calling on the heads of advertising at the largest companies in the world, they won't all talk to you the first day, or the first week, or even the first month.

I especially remember calling one of these advertising directors—Kathy's research with her magnifying glass informed us that they had spent over a quarter of a billion dollars the previous year on advertising. As I dialed the same phone number day after day, I kept reminding myself that we only want a tiny portion of their advertising budget. Finally I wore down all of the gatekeepers, and my prospect answered the phone saying, "Mr. Stovall, I don't know who you are, but do you realize you've called my office fifty-seven days in a row?"

I assured him I was aware of that because Kathy, via her magnifying glass, kept meticulous records of all my calls. I went on to tell him that I was not a pushy salesman, but instead, I was a passionate entrepreneur with a story that I thought was worthy of him and his corporation. They became one of our first advertisers, and that revenue sustained us in the early stages of the Narrative Television Network.

It's important to remember we had a specific plan and worked it diligently without fail. Calling fifty-six days in a row would not have worked and would have resulted in failure. It was that fifty-seventh call that made the difference. There are no moral victories in entrepreneurship. At a certain point, you either succeed or fail, and we keep score with dollars.

Trading Time for Money

Working is trading time for money. Entrepreneurship is creating something that generates money. Remembering Stovall's 11th Commandment—thou shalt not kid thyself—is important here. At a certain point in your entrepreneurial venture, if you can't pay someone to perform the tasks you do on a daily basis, you don't really have a business, you have simply created a job for yourself. Many entrepreneurs fall into the trap of always working in their business and never working on their business.

At some point you have to step away from the daily grind and take a high altitude look at your business. You always have to be creating and re-creating a bigger and better machine. Otherwise, you simply have a job working for yourself instead of working for someone else. Your business must generate profit beyond the value of your own efforts.

Initial Funding

Since we keep score with money, it's important to look at initial funding to begin your venture. I will admit to a bias here in that I prefer to bootstrap ventures without any outside funding whenever it is possible. I have seen countless good ideas that never saw the light of day because the would-be entrepreneurs never found anyone to capitalize their ideas.

There's a reason that venture capitalists are often referred to as "vulture" capitalists. They want a lot of control and equity in your venture in exchange for some up-front cash. In many cases, initial capitalization is more of a convenience than a necessity. While it may seem nice to have the cash on hand today, it comes with a huge price tag and a lot of strings attached tomorrow.

I received a call from an entrepreneur who had read one of my books. He was trying to figure out a way to come up with a little over $2 million in cash. When I inquired what he needed the money for, he told me it was to pay off his accountant. I was shocked and asked how on earth he ran up a $2 million bill with his CPA. He told me about launching his company when cash was tight. Instead of paying a standard accounting bill, he gave up 10 percent of the equity in his venture to save a few thousand dollars in setup costs and regular payroll accounting fees. What seems cheap and insignificant today, may cost you dearly in the future.

There are a lot of crowd-sourced funding opportunities where you can raise significant amounts of capital without giving up any of your equity. You are simply pre-selling enhanced versions of your product or service. You don't give up any of your company, and you don't have to pay the money back.

Some partners and I raised almost a million dollars to do post-production on a movie through crowd-sourced funding. This was accomplished by offering packages of movie posters, DVDS, books, and memorabilia connected to the film. It was little more than a pre-release marketing campaign that netted us a million dollars we didn't have to pay back while keeping all of the ownership in the movie property.

One reason new entrepreneurs feel they need outside capital is so that they can take a sizeable salary out of the business. This may keep you from launching your venture or may cut deeply into your future profits in exchange for a little comfort and convenience today. As in many arenas of life, delayed gratification is a big key to success in entrepreneurship.

I am a huge fan of the side-hustle concept through which entrepreneurs can launch their venture part-time while still maintaining their full-time job. This allows them to pay the bills while they're working out the bugs in their new business. After a few consecutive months of success, they can then entertain the idea of leaving their day job behind. This sacrifice of time, effort, and sleep in the form of sweat equity in your venture can literally be worth millions of dollars in the future. You don't have to have all the bells and whistles when you launch your business.

Start Where You Are

At the Stovall Center for Entrepreneurship, I often remind college students that some of the largest corporations in the world today began in dorm rooms. You can start right where you are. One of the best ways to truly become successful is to avoid trying to act like you already are by surrounding yourself with a false façade purchased with investors' money.

Being an entrepreneur is hard, challenging, and frustrating particularly in the beginning. Using borrowed or invested money to be able to look like you're already successful may keep you from the reality of becoming successful. During our parents' generation, oftentimes people who weren't doing anything but wanted to pretend that they were successful, labeled themselves as "consultants." Today, many people who live in their mom's basement and function in a make-believe world, call themselves "entrepreneurs." An entrepreneur is not what you talk about, it's what you do and who you are.

Kathy and I, as the blind leading the blind, began our television network utilizing borrowed equipment set up in the basement of a condominium in Tulsa, Oklahoma—which is still my beloved hometown, but it is certainly not the entertainment capital of the universe. Since neither of us had any training, background, or experience in the business, we did the best we could with what we had.

Kathy used her big magnifying glass to try to decipher the operating manual for the borrowed video production equipment. I became the first narrator and recorded the soundtracks myself in a tiny studio I made out of a broom closet underneath the stairs that led into the basement. I hung old boat cushions in the broom closet to give us a good studio sound.

If you're considering a career change, and want to be a narrator, the only thing you have to do is read the script and watch the screen until the moment it's time to say your line. But if you're a blind guy like me, and you can't see the screen or read the script, you have to try to memorize the lines, rush into your studio (formerly the broom closet), listen in your headset until you think it's time to speak your lines, and hope for the best.

Initially, it was a time-consuming, frustrating disaster. I will never forget the day when I struggled down the stairs into our basement studio, and Kathy confronted me stating, "I have a new technological breakthrough we are going to start utilizing in our production process beginning today." When I inquired about it, she explained that we were wasting too much time because I never knew exactly when to say my lines since I couldn't watch the screen.

She went on to describe how she had cut the handle off one of the brooms that I had taken out of the closet when I converted it into our studio. She had drilled a hole in the door large enough for the broom handle to fit through, so she instructed, "Now all you have to do is sit there in the broom closet, and when it's time to deliver your line, I'll stab you in the back with this broomstick."

As laughable and pathetic as our method was, we produced programming out of that studio for all of the major broadcast and cable networks, as well as the top movie studios. Our broomstick studio productions proved to be good enough to earn us an Emmy Award.

When aspiring entrepreneurs from around the world call me today and complain that they can't start their venture because they don't have investment capital to afford the best facilities, furniture, and equipment as well as qualified staff, I am really hard to convince. I tell them to find a basement with a closet and look for a broomstick.

When you are striving for success as an entrepreneur, the what, how, when, or where is not as important as why. If you can attach a burning desire to your passion and keep those you serve in the forefront of your mind, you can succeed beyond your wildest dreams. We do everything in life to gain pleasure or avoid pain.

Effort and Attitude

The seed of my success as an entrepreneur began in a grocery store checkout line as I was struggling to begin my journey. Crystal and I would go to the grocery store each week with all of the money we could afford to spend in my pocket. She always brought her calculator with her and would add up the cost of the items we were purchasing as we placed them in our cart. As soon as the calculator told us we had reached the level of the amount of money I had in my pocket, we knew we were going to have to get by with what was in the cart until next week.

On one fateful occasion, we somehow had miscalculated and didn't have enough money. So right there in front of the checkout clerk and the other people in line, Crystal had to go put a loaf of bread back on the shelf. Something about the idea of this beloved person who had helped me complete my education and had always believed in me as an entrepreneur having to put a loaf of bread back on the shelf caused me to forevermore change my mindset.

Standing in the checkout line of that grocery store that day, I committed that I never wanted to have that feeling of scarcity, lack, and failure again. That feeling and image remained so vivid in my mind and spirit as I was launching my entrepreneurial ventures, I was willing to undertake any effort and make any sacrifice in order to achieve success.

If you will find your own reason for succeeding, all of the other details will take care of themselves. The only things we can control are our effort and our attitude.

CHAPTER EIGHT

Learn to Fail–Don't Fail to Learn

by Dr. Kevin Schneider

I am writing this chapter for myself. I am a type A personality, an achiever—and I hate failure. Over the course of my life, I have feared failure, avoided failure, and been deeply discouraged because of failure. But through it all, I eventually learned to learn from failure. How do you view failure? Do you view it as a dead end or closed door? Are you terrified of it? Like an ex-girlfriend or boyfriend, do you run at the sight of it? Do you cringe at the thought failure? Or, do you view it as a process of learning, a way to discover new opportunities, and expected bumps on the road to success? How we handle failure greatly depends on how we view failure, and we must learn that failure is not a monster to be feared but a mentor to be embraced.

Traditionally we have been taught that failure is a bad thing, and it is to be avoided at all costs. While no one actively seeks failure for the mere joy of failing, many entrepreneurial leaders have begun to embrace a more positive paradigm of failure. This is partly because failure is part of life. It is inevitable. However, we need to understand that failure is not the end of the world. In fact, it may be the beginning of something great! Failure is a valuable teacher—if we will listen, if we will allow failure to teach us. I am not saying failure is fun. I don't personally enjoy failing. But I have learned to glean all I can from each failure whether large or small.

Of course, you don't have to take my word for it. Thomas Edison is perhaps the greatest inventor in American history. He is credited with developing more than 1,000 patents, and some of his most noteworthy inventions include the automatic telegraph, carbon telephone transmitter, light bulb, phonograph (record player), movie camera, and alkaline storage battery.[1] As a voracious learner, Edison is famously quoted as saying, "I have not failed 10,000 times. I have not failed once. I have succeeded in proving that those 10,000 ways will not work. When I have eliminated the ways that will not work, I will find the way that will work."[2] I cannot even conceive of failing at something 10,000 times. Yet not only did it take 10,000 prototypes to successfully develop the light bulb, but Edison did not believe that each of these attempts was a failure. He viewed his efforts as a necessary part of a learning process.

The Fear Factor

The late, great Nelson Mandela, South Africa's first Black president, said, "I learned that courage was not the absence of fear, but the triumph over it. The brave man is not he who does not feel afraid, but he who conquers that fear." Every entrepreneur deals with fear—we all do. However, if entrepreneurs are to learn from failure, they must be able to understand and effectively manage their fears.

In *Think and Grow Rich*, Napoleon Hill describes six basic fears and suggests that fear of poverty is the most destructive because it undermines creativity, halts initiative, and destroys purpose and enthusiasm. Hill suggests that the majority of people tend to believe that they fear nothing. It is not that people are necessarily in self-denial, but rather the presence of fear is often subtle and goes unnoticed. As a result, it may take some soul searching and honest self-analysis.

Hill recommends looking for certain symptoms to understand how fear may be impacting our lives. Fear frequently expresses itself through negative emotions such as doubt and worry. Other symptoms of fear can include indifference, indecision, and procrastination. In other words, unidentified and unrestrained fear can be a formidable force inhibiting would-be entrepreneurs from getting started and taking risks.

According to a Harvard study of 65 entrepreneurs in the UK and Canada, researchers found that fear can both inhibit and motivate entrepreneurs. They defined the fear of failure as "a temporary cognitive and emotional reaction to a threat to potential achievement." Similar to Hill's perspective, the Harvard researchers viewed fear as a state rather than inherent personality trait. The study identified seven sources of fear including: financial security; ability to fund the venture; personal ability/self-esteem; potential of the idea; threats to social esteem; the venture's ability to execute; and opportunity costs. Whether fear deterred or motivated the entrepreneur depended on the source.

For example, fear pertaining to financial security, ability to secure funding, and opportunity costs motivated entrepreneurs to persist with the venture. Alternatively, the study found that entrepreneurs were negatively impacted when they worried about the potential of their idea or their personal ability to successfully launch a venture. These entrepreneurs tended to succumb to analysis paralysis and struggled with decision-making in an effort to avoid making a wrong decision. They got bogged down talking about the decision instead of taking action.[3]

The study also provides entrepreneurs with several important insights for making the fear of failure work in their favor. One strategy for harnessing the positive potential of the fear of failure is developing emotional intelligence (EI). People with strong EI are able to understand how they feel, control their emotions, and effectively motivate themselves. For instance, partic- ipants in the Harvard study discussed how they have learned anxiety is temporary and fluctuations in mood impact how they perceive the outcome of their endeavors.

As entrepreneurs develop emotional intelligence, they can reduce the impact of negative emotions asso- ciated with fear. Another method for responding to fear is proactively engaging in problem solving. When fear elicits concern with their venture, entrepreneurs should not ignore the problem. Instead, they should take action to address the underlying issues.

Seeking support through mentors and other advisors is a third approach entrepreneurs can take to combat the fear of failure. Often times other people have the answers to our problems and can provide encour- agement to overcome worry and self-doubt. Finally, continual learning is a powerful strategy that enables entrepreneurs to overcome fear by improving skills and abilities while reducing uncertainty.[4]

Go or Give Up?

Deciding whether and when to give up is one of the hardest decisions entrepreneurs have to make because giving up means admitting failure, and we are hardwired to avoid failure at all costs. There are no bulletproof answers for entrepreneurs facing this tough decision, and the prospect of failure can elicit endless questions. Some questions may hold us back from moving forward with our venture like, "How will my idea ever work?" or, "Should I just go get a job?" Other questions can inspire us to continue such as, "How could I go this far only to give up?" or, "How much will I regret this decision if I give up now?"

As with many other areas in our life, the inner narrative we listen to will likely determine the path we choose to travel. And we need to consider that although we may have failed once, or many times, this does not mean the venture cannot ultimately end in success.

R.U. Darby was an insurance salesman who once launched out in a speculative venture with his uncle hoping to strike gold during the California gold rush. His uncle staked a claim to a parcel of land in California and immediately began digging. Although the backbreaking work was arduous and slow, he persisted until he eventually struck gold. Needing costly machinery to mine the ore, he buried the mine to go back home and the raise capital required to purchase the equipment.

Excited by the prospects of riches, friends and family pitched in until Darby raised the needed investment. Before long, he was shipping carts of ore to the smelters and earning great returns on his investment. However, as quickly as the mine was discovered, it suddenly disappeared. Subsequent drilling yielded no sign of the vein of gold, so Darby and his uncle junked the equipment and gave up the search.[5]

The junkman who purchased the machinery was curious to explore whether the mine really had no gold. He hired a mining engineer to look at the mine and do some analysis. The engineer suggested that the mysterious disappearance of ore in Darby's mine was not because the mine ran dry. He believed the Darby's failed because they did not understand fault lines. In fact, the junkman's engineer's calculations revealed the vein of gold may be just three feet from where the Darbys stopped drilling. And this is exactly where the junkman struck gold—just three feet from where the Darbys had failed.[6]

Like Darby, success may just be a few steps beyond the point where we give up and declare failure. Before you throw in the towel on an entrepreneurial venture, ask yourself, "Am I three feet from gold?" Just think if Steve Jobs, Jeff Bezos, or Elon Musk had given up during the very difficult early years. Where would we be without iPhones, Amazon Prime Now, or sleek electric cars? Life just wouldn't be the same! If you don't give up on your dreams, you may find that your idea has the potential to change the world.

To achieve success, entrepreneurs must persist, fight through the doubts, and maintain a never-give-up attitude. However, there are times when an idea has run its course, the money runs out, or you come across better opportunities. It may be that your idea will never be a profitable business, or it simply could mean that the idea won't work in its current form. Your idea might even be ahead of its time, and current technology or infrastructure need to advance before you are able to launch the venture. There are also intrinsic factors that may signal it is time to admit failure, quit, and move on.

For instance, many entrepreneurs who have labored hard to bring a dream to life continue to struggle year after year and begin to face burnout. Other entrepreneurs, initially excited about an idea, come to realize they have lost their passion for the business and no longer feel fulfilled by the venture.

Although you may abandon an idea, cut a product, or even close a business, this doesn't mean you are a failure. Failure is part of the entrepreneurial process of innovating and creating new things. It simply may be time for a pivot.

Stay Lean!

The traditional entrepreneurial paradigm typically includes something similar to the following approach. An entrepreneur has an idea. She dreams, thinks, and researches everything she can about the idea. Friends and family provide positive feedback and encourage the entrepreneur to move forward with starting a business. A months-long business planning process commences with management and marketing plans created and financial statements forecasted. The business plan is presented to banks and early potential investors. The entrepreneur sources material suppliers and a manufacturer to develop the product.

After an initial version is developed, the product is produced and sold through traditional brick and mortar or online channels. The process is relatively the same for launching a service-based company except that the manufacturing and physical products are replaced by service packages and offerings. Once the products start selling, the profits start rolling in, right? As any entrepreneur will tell you, it's not exactly that easy.

According to the U.S. Bureau of Labor Statistics, around half of all business fail within five years and nearly two-thirds failure within ten years.[7] If the business planning process for launching a new venture is straightforward, why have failure rates for new businesses remained so high for decades? In *The Startup Owner's Manual: The Step-by-Step Guide for Building a Great Company,* Steve Blank and Bob Dorf provide some important insights that explain this phenomenon. They argue that a startup is not simply a smaller version of a larger company. Rather, it is a "temporary organization in search of a scalable, repeatable, profitable business model."

In other words, a well-written business plan tends to provide an appearance that the entrepreneur already has a scalable, profitable business model. He just needs startup capital to execute the plan, and the financial projections reveal how the profits will grow. However, this is typically not the case with startups. In fact, business plans are just a collection of unproven assumptions that rarely survive first contact with customers.[8]

Blank and Dorf advise that entrepreneurs take an entirely different approach for launching startups that reduces the likelihood of failure through flipping the startup process on its head. Instead of developing extensive business plans, entrepreneurs should use the business model canvas developed by Alex Osterwalder. The canvas contains nine basic cells that include the value proposition, customer segments, customer relationships, channels, key partners, key activities, key resources, cost structure, and revenue streams.[9] It is a dynamic tool used for creating and testing hypotheses in the search for a repeatable, scalable business model. As entrepreneurs develop hypotheses, they are required to get out of the building to test assumptions by interviewing potential customers. Ideas and assumptions frequently fail as entrepreneurs interact with customers, but this process allows startups to fail fast and fail often. This lean approach is a vast departure from the more static business planning process.[10]

Following lean methods does not make a startup immune to failure. Just the opposite is true. Failure is an integral part of the process. As entrepreneurs search for a repeatable, scalable business model, they are constantly engaged in an iterative loop where failure leads to learning and innovation.

In The Lean Startup: How Today's Entrepreneurs Use Continuous Innovation to Create Radically Successful Businesses, Eric Ries advises that startups make constant adjustments with a steering wheel he calls the "Build-Measure-Learn" feedback loop. Through this adaptive process, entrepreneurs can determine whether to continue along the current path or change directions. Ries describes how this process of learning through failure results in a pivot rather than a dead end. The idea of a pivot in the lean approach comes from the sports world where an athlete changes direction with one foot anchored to the ground. Equipped with this new perspective of failure in the startup world, entrepreneurs should endeavor to fail fast, fail often, and view every failure as an opportunity to learn.[11]

Learn to Learn

The CliftonStrengths Assessment is a 30-minute assessment that includes 177 questions that measures your talents. The assessment analyzes patterns of thinking, feeling, and behaving, and then categorizes strengths into 34 themes that fall within four categories—executing, influencing, relationship building, and strategic thinking.[12]

The first time I took the assessment, my number one strength came back as Learner. I was immediately upset because I thought my number one strength should be something impressive like Command, Futuristic, or

Strategic. Certainly the assessment had either made an error or was inherently flawed. I thought to myself, "What in the world is a Learner talent, and how is this even a strength?"

As I began to research the definition of the person with a Learner talent, it wasn't what I expected. For the Learner, I discovered that the process is more important than the content or result, and the outcome is less significant than simply "getting there."[13] In other words, there is a process to learning. Although it may not be your greatest strength, you can learn to learn.

Also, as we explored in earlier chapters, our view of failure as well as our ability to learn are both impacted by our mindset. We can choose to foster either a growth or fixed mindset. If we choose the growth mindset, then we believe we can continue to learn and grow. However, if we have a fixed mindset, then we will have a very limited view regarding our ability to learn. For example, not only were the participants with a growth mindset in Dweck's study not discouraged by failure, they didn't even know they were failing. They thought they were learning!

Additionally, growth-minded students described how they did not see grades as an end in themselves, but rather as part of the process of learning and discovery. This is a critical, central theme Dweck discovered in her research—the growth mindset actually orients a person toward learning. Thus, entrepreneurs should do all they can to develop a growth mindset to accelerate their ability to learn and overcome failure.[14]

CHAPTER NINE

The Daily Journey

by Jim Stovall

We all love brainstorming sessions where we can dream big and imagine our success. We can create elaborate business plans and set the stage to launch our venture—but at some point we pull the trigger, and it all comes down to performing at a high level within our daily routine. If you want to have a good life, you need to have a good year. If want to have a good year, you need to have a good month. A good month is made up of good weeks, and it all boils down to having a good day today. Yesterday is history, tomorrow is a mystery, and today is a gift which is why we call it the present.

We all know someone, maybe ourselves, who set an aggressive New Year's resolution to work out regularly and get into shape. Stylish workout clothes were purchased, gym memberships were obtained, and everything was ready to go; but within a few short weeks or months, it all ground to a halt. Regardless of what you have imagined, if you don't implement, all your dreams and preparations have been in vain.

As stated earlier, we live in a world that, when it's all said and done, there's a lot more said than done. The entrepreneurs who have made their mark on history are not necessarily those who had the greatest ideas; but in every case, the entrepreneurs who have become household names are those who have taken action and implemented their plan. I believe, among the saddest reality in the human condition is the fact that some of the greatest art, most fabulous music, and world-changing entrepreneurial ideas have gone to the grave as nothing more than ideas inside someone's mind and spirit. I would much rather attempt to do something great and fail than attempt to do nothing and succeed.

I remember my days as an aspiring football player. During one particular practice, we were reviewing the blocking schemes for all of the different formations and variations that the defense might implement. On one particular play, I got up to the line and realized I had no idea which player I was supposed to block. The ball was snapped, the play was run, and our running back was promptly tackled by a defender I was supposed to have blocked. The offensive line coach approached me and inquired in a tone that only upset football coaches can muster, "What in the world was that?"

I explained that, with all the shifts in all the formations, I forgot who I was supposed to block. He gave me a piece of advice then that served me well as a football player and continues to serve me well today as an entrepreneur. He said, "If you're not sure who to block or what to do, do something because doing nothing is never the right course of action. If you block someone, you may get the right guy. But even if you block the wrong person, you get out of the way and we have a chance."

There is no such thing as a perfect plan, and even if you had one, you couldn't implement it perfectly. Action is the key to progress, and progress is the key to success. If you're making sales calls, funding presentations, or doing marketing outreach, your efforts may not always result in a positive outcome, but if you don't at least plant the seed and ask the question, the answer will always be no.

A principle of science tells us that once you begin a repetitive task, the law of averages sets in, and a ratio takes over. I am a huge baseball fan, and during the season you can find me listening to a game on the satellite almost every day. I am convinced that even as a blind person, I could get a hit off of the best pitcher in the Major Leagues if you will allow me to change only one rule in the game of baseball. Instead of only getting three strikes, if you gave me an unlimited number of strikes, sooner or later I will inevitably hit the ball.

Entrepreneurship is not a three-strikes-and-you're-out game. It is, instead, a tryuntil-you-succeed-or-quit proposition. Given this reality, you hold the key to your future.

Productivity

Once you've decided to take action and persist until you achieve success, you have to deal with the concept of productivity. Productivity is simply the process of getting the most you can out of what you have. Productivity dictates that you should be performing tasks within your business that only you can do and where you are the most efficient. As we discussed in a previous chapter, Michael Jordan playing baseball was mediocre, but Michael Jordan playing basketball was legendary. The difference between the two functions defines productivity for Michael Jordan.

In my book *The Art of Productivity*, I broke down the concept of being productive into three elements: motivation, communication, and implementation.

Motivation

Motivation is the first element of productivity, and it controls all of your activities. If you are not motivated by what you do all day every day, you will eventually not be competitive because your competition will be doing things that motivate them. We are all motivated by different things. Some people are motivated by money, others are motivated by titles or recognition, and still others are motivated by the approval of their team. You must come to fully understand what motivates you and everyone in your organization.

Several years ago, I was catching the earliest flight of the day out of my hometown airport. I immediately realized that something was different that particular day from any other day on which I had caught the 6 a.m. flight. Unlike other days, the airport staff was exceedingly polite and professional, everyone was energetic and totally upbeat. My colleague and I were totally baffled as to what had created this amazing change among the airline staff.

As a blind person, I generally pre-board the jet, so as my colleague and I settled into our seats, there was only one other passenger on the plane, and he was sitting right across the aisle from me. I extended my hand and said, "Good morning, I'm Jim Stovall." He shook my hand and responded with his name, and I instantly realized I was talking with the president of the airline, which immediately explained the atmosphere within the airport terminal that morning.

The service on that flight was impeccable, and at one point, several of the flight attendants were gathered around the president of the airline. He asked them how they liked the incentive package he had recently put into place for airline employees. They all responded positively and gave him glowing feedback.

A little later in the flight, I got up to use the restroom and was standing next to the galley where the flight attendants were preparing our meal. The comments among them were quite different from what I had heard them say in front of the airline president. They said, "Can you believe he thinks that program will motivate us," and "It's not only de-motivating, it's embarrassing." As I stood there in the aisle waiting for my turn in the restroom, I realize that at that moment, I knew more about motivating the staff of that airline than the president did.

Often, as the leader of an organization, you are in the worst position to get accurate constructive feedback from your people. Make sure that you look at each member of your team individually. Get to know them and understand what motivates them. If you go into the locker room before any game, you will see players listening to music on their headsets. The music helps them to relax, focus, and get motivated for the game. Some players listen to classical music while others listen to rock, country, or rap. There's no one-size-fits-all answer to motivation.

Communication

The second element of productivity is communication. No matter how motivated you may be, or how exciting the entrepreneurial venture you are pursuing, your ideas and opportunities are no more impactful than your ability to communicate them to your team, your customers, and your prospects. Just as in motivation, there's no one-size-fits-all way to communicate. Some people receive communication best verbally, while others prefer to see it in writing. Some people need to restate the communication back to the presenter in order to fully grasp it, while others learn best from a visual example.

There's a wonderful resort on a small island in Mission Bay off the coast of San Diego, California. Several times a year for over two decades, I have spoken for a worldwide leadership conference there. My colleagues and I always stay in the same bungalows on the beach, and the staff has gotten to know us very well over the years. On one of our trips, the general manager of the resort approached me, welcomed me back, and said, "Mr. Stovall, our staff had a meeting last week and discussed the fact that you get a lot of phone calls while you're with us, but as a blind person, you're not able to see the message light on the phone to know when you've received a call. So, we've come up with plan to accommodate you."

He went on to describe that when someone called for me and I was not available, instead of utilizing the message light on the phone they would dispatch a bellman out to my bungalow and slide message slips under the door. While I really appreciated their thought and effort, to a blind person, message slips you can't read aren't any better than a message light you can't see.

You must open the most efficient channel and avenue of communication between you every person you deal with. There is an optimal way to communicate with anyone on your team, but it won't be the same way for everyone.

Implementation

The final element of productivity is implementation. Regardless of how motivated you may be or how well you may communicate your motivation, unless or until you implement, it is all in vain. Some people are morning people, while others are late night people. Some people focus on one activity while others prefer to multitask. Some people work best alone while others function at their highest level as part of a team. Once again, there's no right or wrong answer for everyone. You have to find the right strategy for each person with whom you deal.

Productivity Profile

Several years ago, I developed a tool to help entrepreneurs and those who lead teams establish the most productive ways to motivate, communicate, and implement with each person in their organization. If you would like to receive this productivity profile for you and your team free of charge, just send an email to Jim@JimStovall.com and put the code 586404 in the subject line.

As you're establishing the elements that will make you the most productive, it is critical that you not confuse activity with productivity. Just because you're doing something doesn't mean you are getting anywhere. Always remember the hamster running on the wheel in the cage. There's a lot of activity and no productivity. If you were to watch cars driving along the highway at the speed limit, you might assume they're making a lot of progress. When in reality, some of them could be going the wrong way, and every minute they're getting farther from their goals and their destination. Doing the wrong thing at the wrong time with the wrong people can be unproductive.

Halting all activity while you get the right plan in place, motivate yourself and everyone involved, and communicate your vision before you implement, is always more productive than moving at top speed in the wrong direction.

Entrepreneurs work in new and different ways than ever before. The emergence of digital commerce has forevermore altered the landscape. It may seem you have to make a choice as to whether you are going to be a digital or traditional business. In reality, virtually all entrepreneurs in the future will be both. Even if you're a brick and mortar operation on the main street of your town, you are likely going to be selling products or buying inventory via the Internet. You are going to be bringing customers into your establishment via the web, and they are going to be rating your business online.

You may think you are a totally digital business, both buying and selling on the web and serving customers around the world you never meet, but your products are going to be delivered via traditional means. You are going to have to deal with packaging, shipping, and delivery even if you outsource this portion of your business. The world's greatest online business can't survive without the traditional delivery of products and services.

Protection Importance

As you are launching and beginning to operate your business, you must protect it in every way. The first and most vital element of entrepreneurship that you must protect is your mind. Your business was launched in your mind and will be sustained through your own positive mental attitude. An entrepreneur may take a day off, but his or her mind never does.

Artists observe light, architects observe construction, and musicians listen to sounds. Entrepreneurs will always be observing opportunities and potential within the marketplace. As a blind person, I experience the world based on who I travel with and the people with whom I associate.

You must protect your attitude based on what you read, what you listen to, and what you watch. But most importantly, you must select who you are going to spend time with. If you accept a job within a corporate structure, you have little or no control over the people you interact with daily. As an entrepreneur, you have to take control of your environment. The only essential ingredients of a successful employee, colleague, or member of your team are effort and attitude. You can teach people how to do anything if they will put forth the right effort and maintain the proper attitude.

However, the most skilled person in the world who has a bad attitude and puts forth no effort will drag you down along with your entire team. It's like the up and down of a seesaw. You have to associate with individuals who have a positive attitude, believe in what you're doing, and are willing to go the extra mile.

After you protect the mental aspects of your business, you have to protect the physical part of your entrepreneurial venture. As we discussed in a previous chapter, you have to have legal, accounting, and insurance advisors around you. These people can eliminate or mitigate the risks that every venture faces. You should never take any risks you don't have to. Every time you make a decision, you're risking the possibility that you make the wrong choice. Never make any decisions until you have to. If you can wait another day, week, or month to finalize a decision without paying a price for that extra time, wait until the last minute. This will give you more time to think about it and seek counsel. The prevailing conditions may change before you have to make a critical decision.

The most important element you must protect in your entrepreneurial venture is your good name and the name of your company. My friend and mentor, legendary Coach John Wooden, told me, "You'll be known for a lifetime of great things you do, or for one lapse in judgment." We all know people or organizations that were at the top of their game until one avoidable, ridiculous lapse in judgment took it all away. In the world of high-speed communication and connectivity, everyone will know everything you do instantaneously.

Too often, people think of entrepreneurs as fringe people who are wheeler/dealers, riverboat gamblers, or scam artists. In reality, the entrepreneurs who succeed over the long haul are those who form win-win relationships. Whether it's a colleague, a supplier, or a customer, unless a deal is good for everyone, it's not really good for anyone. Never burn any bridges as an entrepreneur because you don't know when you're going to need to cross the same river again. People do business with who they know and who they're comfortable with. Be the kind of entrepreneur that you would want to do business with.

High quality research will protect you from making uninformed or ill-timed decisions, but when doing research, it is critical to look at what people do as opposed to just listening to what they say. If you ask your friends and family what they think of your entrepreneurial idea, you will get a variety of answers born out of a variety of motivations. The best research is done when a paying customer is ready, willing, and able to let go of hard-earned dollars.

The final area of entrepreneurship that you need to protect and nurture is yourself. Everyone who gets a

job goes to work in an existing organization, but entrepreneurs begin only with themselves including their
thoughts, dreams, and ideas. I consult with many entrepreneurs who want to be more successful. Oftentimes,
after examining how they operate, I give them the ironic
advice, "Instead of trying to work harder or smarter, you
need to work less."

In the movie, *The Ultimate Gift*, based on my novel,
the esteemed actor Brian Dennehy brought to life one of
my favorite characters named Gus Caldwell. Gus Caldwell was the quintessential Texas rancher and oilman.
In the story, he found himself called upon to mentor
a spoiled, self-centered young man. After teaching the
young man to work hard and take pride in his accom-
plishments, Gus tells his protégé, "It's time to quit for
the day." The young man protests, explaining that he just
wanted to finish one last section of fence. Gus's response
to him also will serve entrepreneurs. He said, "Work on
a ranch is never done."

There will always be more to do and still more do
after that, but never forget that the reason you wanted to
become an entrepreneur was to experience more of life
and experience it deeper. If you don't balance your entrepreneurship with your kids' ballgames, the school plays,
fishing with your dad, and your anniversary dinner, you
have failed as an entrepreneur and as a person.

CHAPTER TEN

Go for Grit

by Dr. Kevin Schneider

There are few application processes more rigorous than that of the United States Military Academy at West Point. With an acceptance rate around 10 percent, admission to West Point is extremely selective. Not only are stellar high school grades and top scores on standardized exams such as the ACT and SAT required, but applicants must also secure a nomination from a US Representative, Senator, or even the President of the United States. And by the way, you must be between the ages of 17 and 23 and pass a rigorous fitness assessment that includes timed running, pull-ups, sit-ups, and push-ups.

If you are one of the few who meet all of the requirements and are accepted into the academy, the next hurdle you face is an intensive seven-week training called Beast Barracks. The Beast includes nonstop military training, classroom instruction, and organized athletics, and it is known as the most physically and emotionally demanding time at West Point.[1]

Although the admissions process is designed to select the men and women with the highest potential for successfully graduating West Point, the Beast Barracks are so intense that many new cadets drop out within the first few months of the academy. This begs the question: What would cause so many new cadets to drop out so quickly after successfully making it through such an extensive admissions process?

US Army researchers had been asking this very question for decades without a conclusive answer. That is, until Angela Duckworth's research unlocked the answer. She discovered that the admissions Whole Candidate Score—which is the primary tool used to evaluate candidates for entrance into West Point—did not reliably predict which cadets would successfully make it through the Beast Barracks. Through this revelation, Duckworth found that fierce determination rather than raw talent was the underlying factor that distinguished the successful cadets.[2]

The Talent Trap

In the US, we tend to be obsessed with talent. Whether it is a sports icon, movie star, or business mogul, Americans love stories about wonderfully talented people. This reality is reflected in TV shows such as American

Idol and America's Got Talent. We tend to idolize "overnight" success stories and are tempted to think that talent provides us with a fast track to success, fame, and wealth. In Angela Duckworth's book, *Grit: The Power of Passion and Perseverance*, she defines this "naturalness bias" as "a hidden prejudice against those who've achieved what they have because they worked for it, and a hidden preference for those whom we think arrived at their place in life because they're naturally talented."

However, talent does not provide the whole picture when it comes to achievement. When Duckworth was teaching math class, she often found that several of her most talented students were not earning the best grades. On the other hand, many struggling students would end up scoring better than she had anticipated. She eventually discovered that intellectual talent did guarantee academic success.[3]

As a professor, I have found this doesn't change much at the university level. The general academic bar may be higher, but the outcomes of talent versus effort play out in similar fashion. For instance, initially identifying the very brightest students is usually not difficult. Year after year I have often noticed how students' ability to quickly learn concepts or share keen insights did not necessarily correlate with academic achievement. All of the most talented students did not earn the top grades, and some of them ended up performing poorly. I also observed that there were students who exhibited less raw talent in my courses but would often perform very well. In fact, I recall several struggling students who were incredibly hard workers. Although they were initially underperformers, they ended up with respectable grades through great effort and determination.

One of the hardest working, most determined people I have ever met was one of my roommates in college, and I ended up choosing him as the best man in my wedding. His father had been in the military, and he was a wrestler for many years. He was physically and mentally tough, and he had a never-give-up attitude that I had never seen before. He was intelligent but had his challenges academically. While there were some exceptionally bright students in our MBA program, he struggled through several courses and even had to repeat a couple classes. He successfully completed the program, but he did not win any of the awards or gain any particular recognition.

Although he didn't receive the academic accolades, I knew he was destined for significant success. He certainly believed he was going to do something great, and I had seen how he was willing to outwork the smartest students to successfully complete his MBA. The last time I spoke with him he was leading a global, multibillion-dollar technology merger for an international payments company, and I believe he is just tapping into the potential success he will achieve during his lifetime.

Grit Trumps Talent

Duckworth's research reveals that grit, not talent, is the best indicator of success. She defines grit as a combination of passion and perseverance. In addition, Duckworth discovered that grit is not fixed; we can develop grit through experience and effort. Through years of research, she developed the Grit Scale. This instrument separates talent from grit, and it asks a variety of questions to measure a person's level of passion and perseverance. In order to measure perseverance, the scale includes questions that pertain to finishing what you start and overcoming challenges that you face when attempting to accomplish something important. Questions to gauge passion include measuring how often interests change as well as how long you might stick with, or even obsess over, an idea or project.[4]

Professionals from a variety of fields have taken the test over the years, and the Grit Scale has produced consistent results regardless of the sector or career category. From military personnel to educators to salespeople, grit predicted who remained and who dropped out. It accurately predicted who would stick with their commitments as well as company metrics such as retention rates. Not only was there no correlation between grit and talent, but grit was also a better predictor of success in each case. In one educational study, grit was even inversely correlated with IQ. Although other characteristics are important in a given field such as prior experience, physical fitness, or a support network, grit still matters the most. In addition, grit is not static; it can change over time. In other words, we may have natural talent and great potential, but what we do with it over the course of our lives makes all the difference.[5]

Discover Your Purpose: A Job or Calling?

If grit is a better indicator of success than talent, how do we develop grit? Building up on Duckworth's research, Caroline Adams Miller suggests that the Japanese concept of ikigia lies at the center of grit. Ikigai can be translated as "that which I wake up for."[6] What we wake up for is what drives us. It is what gives our lives meaning and purpose, and finding our purpose is a key element in igniting our passions. When we find our ikigai, it provides the intrinsic motivation we need to pursue our passions. Purpose and passion help sustain us while pursuing challenging goals while potentially facing years of setbacks. Thus, in addition to passion and perseverance, finding your purpose is also an important part of developing grit.

What is your reason for existence? Why were you put on this earth? What do you want written in your eulogy after you have passed from this earth? Although these and other similar questions may require extensive soul searching, they are important to answer if we want to discover our purpose and develop grit. Most of us can readily describe what we do. However, our purpose does not simply describe what we do; it is the underlying reason to why we do it. Purpose acts as a North Star that helps determine the direction for our lives, and it guides our decision-making. It provides the impetus for action and ignites our passion.

One way we can evaluate the extent to which we have discovered our purpose is determining whether we view what we do as a job, a career, or a calling. If the main impetus for me showing up at work every day is collecting a paycheck, I have a job. There is absolutely nothing wrong with this. We all need to earn a living through honest work. However, I am probably not very committed to the work I do if all I have is a job.

If I am pursuing a career in medicine, finance, or law, then I am probably a lot more committed to my work because I am likely interested in advancement as I work my way up the corporate ladder. There are often many competing motivations, but people do not typically pursue a career just to collect a paycheck.

A calling is very different from a job or career. A calling emanates from our purpose. Instead of a means to personal achievement, it is a drive to impact the world.

In the world of entrepreneurship, there is an increasing interest in launching a startup not just as a way to earn an income, but also as a means to impact peoples' lives. Referred to as social entrepreneurship, this growing field has exploded over the last two decades. These purpose-driven entrepreneurs often champion causes such as poverty alleviation, education, and environmental sustainability. Unlike traditional nonprofits, social entrepreneurs seek to change the world through profit-oriented business ventures. Their focus is not only on developing products and serving customers, but they search for ways to empower marginalized communities and improve the environment. As social innovators balance profit with positively impacting people and the planet, their business goals are motivated by a greater overarching purpose to make the world a better place.

Harness Your Passion

To ignite passion, interest usually comes first. You first harness passion through inherently enjoying what you do. Not that you will find every detail thrilling about a particular field or endeavor, but you will enjoy many or most aspects if you have a passion for it. You don't have to enjoy every detail, but fascination for an idea stokes passion to get started. Passion, however, is not just something that you enjoy or something that makes you happy. It certainly does include these positive emotions, but it is more than that. The kind of passion that produces grit results in consistent action over time as you pursue the same big picture goal. In other words, your passion serves your purpose.

For instance, one passion item on the Grit Scale measures our capacity to work with distant objects in view, and our ability to work toward a definite goal. Although we may begin an endeavor out of excitement, it is ultimately passion that will keep us focused on the venture over the long haul.[7]

Just how important is developing a passion for what we do? People perform much better at work when they do what they love. They also miss work less often and stay longer at the same company. For instance, according to Gallup surveys on employee engagement, just over a third of employees are engaged at work while 14 percent are actively disengaged. This means the vast majority of people are not passionately connected to the work they do, and many are psychologically unattached to their work and company.

Unengaged employees typically provide minimum effort required for the job and are often on the look-out for better employment opportunities, while their engaged counterparts are more productive and experience much greater well-being. The Gallup polls have ultimately found that business units scoring in the top half on employee engagement more than double their chances for success compared to those in the bottom half of the survey.[8]

Although the rate of employee disengagement in the workplace is alarming, it appears that their entre-preneurial counterparts often exude greater levels of passion. In the context of entrepreneurship, passion can generally be defined as "…enthusiasm, joy, and even zeal that come from the energetic and unflagging pursuit of a worthy, challenging, and uplifting purpose."[9] It can also be defined as "an entrepreneur's intense affective state accompanied by cognitive and behavioral manifestations of high personal value." Passion lies at the heart of entrepreneurship, and it is one of the most frequently observed characteristics of entrepreneurs.

For instance, passion often plays a central role as entrepreneurs creatively conceive ideas and persuade other people to support a new venture with their time, resources, and talent. Passion is fundamental to the entrepreneurial process because it is a strong indicator of the entrepreneur's level of commitment, ability to articulate a vision, and capacity to effectively lead the venture.[10]

Harnessing passion can also provide the drive needed for entrepreneurs to work grueling hours during the startup and growth phases of a venture. Entrepreneurs face a range of challenges over the course of the life cycle of the new startup such as insufficient knowledge and limited resources. In addition, entrepreneurs assume various demanding roles such as inventing new products and services, founding a new organization, and building a successful company.[11]

Given the level of uncertainty and many challenges surrounding launching new ventures, passion is often a key driver of entrepreneurial action. Passion is important for entrepreneurs not only because it provides meaning and purpose to everyday work, but it also fuels motivation to overcome insurmountable barriers. In other words, entrepreneurs harness passion to meet challenges head-on and overcome difficulties.[12]

Unrelenting Perseverance

If a combination of purpose and passion are one side of the grit coin, then perseverance is the other side. And given the incredible array of challenges entrepreneurs face, it is probably accurate to say that perseverance is one of the most important qualities they must develop. For instance, if you can imagine a person who must communicate a vision for ideas that seem incredulous, create solutions to problems that appear impossible, develop markets where none exist, raise money from wealthy money managers to invest in a dream, and lead and inspire a team to keep going in the face of great difficulty, then you have just described the quintessential entrepreneur. Entrepreneurs keep going when others falter for fear and when most would have given up.

In one of his most famous speeches, Theodore Roosevelt said:

> It is not the critic who counts; not the man who points out how the strong man stumbles, or where the doer of deeds could have done them better. The credit belongs to the man who is actually in the arena, whose face is marred by

dust and sweat and blood; who strives valiantly; who errs, who comes short again and again, because there is no effort without error and shortcoming; but who does actually strive to do the deeds; who knows great enthusiasms, the great devotions; who spends himself in a worthy cause; who at the best knows in the end the triumph of high achievement, and who at the worst, if he fails, at least fails while daring greatly, so that his place shall never be with those cold and timid souls who neither know victory nor defeat.

This quote rings true for entrepreneurs. Often criticized, entrepreneurs persevere regardless of the circumstances. They find a way where others don't see a path forward.

Take Steve Jobs, for example. Jobs is one of the greatest entrepreneurs of our era. He will always be remembered for creating iconic products including the iPod, iPhone, and iPad, and ultimately building one of the most valuable companies in history. Many people, however, may not realize there was a time when Jobs was fired from his own company and Apple Computer almost went bankrupt. Jobs had every reason to give up after Apple fired him, but he refused to admit defeat. In fact, Jobs believed getting fired from Apple was one of the greatest things that ever happened to him. It was during this hiatus from Apple that he founded other companies such as NeXT, a software company, and Pixar, the studio that pioneered computer animation and produced some of the greatest animated movies of all time such as *Toy Story, Finding Nemo,* and *Cars.*

Before returning to Apple as CEO in 1997, Jobs said:

> I'm convinced that about half of what separates the successful entrepreneurs from the non-successful ones is pure perseverance. It is so hard and you pour so much of your life into this thing, there are such rough moments in time that most people give up. And I don't blame them, it's really tough.[13]

Although the entrepreneurial road is windy and rife with difficultly, the research clearly shows that perseverance pays off. For instance, it is a common misperception that young people tend to be the most successful entrepreneurs, and this view is reinforced by cases of some of the most famous entrepreneurs such as Bill Gates, Steve Jobs, and Mark Zuckerberg. While young entrepreneurs do enjoy some advantages, older entrepreneurs often have greater access to human, social, and financial capital. The evidence indicates that founders who are middle-aged and beyond are more successful than their younger counterparts, and the mean founder age for the highest growth ventures is 45 years old. In fact, a

50-year-old founder is 1.8 times more likely to achieve high growth compared to a founder who is age 30.[14]

Whether we glean from the stories of great entrepreneurs or learn from leading academic research, it is important we understand that entrepreneurship is a marathon, not a sprint.

CHAPTER ELEVEN

The Legacy Journey

by Jim Stovall

I am convinced that entrepreneurship can bring you anything and everything you ever wanted in your life for yourself and for your family; but over time you will discover that it's not enough. At some point, in order to sustain your entrepreneurial efforts, you have to find something bigger than yourself and your personal desires. While there's nothing wrong with Learjets, limousines, vacation homes, and everything that goes along with wealth and success, you need to have your true long-term passion wrapped up in a cause or a project that makes the world a better place.

My million-dollar gift that was born out of a commitment I made when I only had ten dollars to my name was not the end, instead, it is just the beginning. Through the Stovall Center for Entrepreneurship, it's my goal to help a thousand young people around the world start businesses and make their own million-dollar gifts to causes that matter to them. In this way, over the next few decades, one thousand of these million-dollar gifts will turn into a billion dollars that will have grown out of a ten-dollar bill, a dream, and a lot of hard work.

The first part of your entrepreneurial legacy involves launching your venture and building your business with excellence and integrity. When I enter my office each day, my first priority is the people like you who read my books as well as those who watch our movies, TV shows, and educational programs; audiences who listen to my speeches; those worldwide who read my columns in newspapers, magazines, and online publications; and listeners who hear me on the radio. If you don't take care of your customers or clients first, nothing else matters.

My second priority is my team, made up of colleagues who make it possible for me to do what I do. I am committed to creating an environment in which they can each meet their personal and professional goals. I want all of my teammates to be able to pursue their passions and be able to become financially independent within our organization.

My third and last priority when I come to work each day is myself. I realize that if I take care of my customers and my colleagues, I will be taken care of beyond my wildest dreams. Entrepreneurship is not just a matter of making money so that you can go do good things.

Performing your tasks within your business is a way you contribute to everyone and give back to the world.

We have a foundation that supports a number of charity and nonprofit causes, but few, if any of them, do as much good work in the world as we do at the Narrative Television Network in helping blind people enjoy movies and television as well as helping visually impaired students get their education within a mainstream environment. Whether you manufacture snow tires, sell insurance, own a restaurant, or pursue virtually any other endeavor, dealing with those you serve with excellence is the most important part of your legacy.

After writing several nonfiction books, I tried my hand at writing a novel. That first effort became the book, *The Ultimate Gift* that was turned into the first of a number of movies based on my novels. After the movie was produced, but before it was released in more than one thousand theaters across the country, I was very proud of my movie partners and our distribution partner, Twentieth Century Fox, when they all agreed to a pre-release strategy that allowed charities and nonprofit organizations to have private screenings of *The Ultimate Gift*, at no cost, as a way to raise funds and build momentum within their organizations.

I was elated that we held more than 300 of these charitable screenings in the months leading up to the theatrical release of *The Ultimate Gift* movie. I remain proud and humbled that the charitable screenings of *The Ultimate Gift* raised in excess of $27 million—every penny of which stayed in those local communities with the charities that hosted the movie premieres. While our intentions were totally humanitarian in our pre-release movie screening strategy, ironically, the charitable events created a lot of publicity that really helped when *The Ultimate Gift* opened in theaters across the country. Good work is its own reward, but it often pays unexpected dividends.

Frontier Entrepreneurship

One of the most exciting aspects of our work at the Stovall Center for Entrepreneurship is a concept Dr. Schneider calls "frontier entrepreneurship." This is the concept of exporting the principals and success strategies to envision, launch, and run successful businesses around the world. You've heard it said that if you give a person a fish, they eat for a day, but if you teach them to fish, they eat for a lifetime. While this is true, when you take the concept a bit further, if you teach people how to teach fishing or give them opportunities in a fishing business, you can feed countless people for generations.

Each year at the Stovall Center for Entrepreneurship, we host a launch competition in which college students plan and start real businesses in the real world. A wonderful business that won the launch competition in the most recent year, as I write these words, is a company called Ichtus that provides opportunities and a free and fair marketplace for independent fisherman in Central America.

Ali from Somalia

One of the greatest examples I have ever witnessed of exporting entrepreneurship comes from my friend Ali who lives in San Diego, California. I met Ali approximately twenty years ago on one of the several trips I take each year to an island in Mission Bay to speak at an international leadership conference. Ali was the cab driver who picked up my colleague and me at the San Diego airport and took us to the island.

During the ride I asked him about himself, and he told me he had arrived in the United States as a refugee from Somalia. We talked about my business, what I would be speaking about at the event, and I gave him several of my books. I enjoyed chatting with him, so I made arrangements for him to pick us up for our return trip to the airport in a few days, and we called Ali for all of our ground transportation in San Diego for many years.

About three years after that first ride, Ali picked us up at the airport in a limousine. When I asked about it, he told me he still owned his cab and had purchased several other cabs, but now he was expanding into the limousine business. Our friendship grew over the course of each of my trips, and we shared ideas about success and entrepreneurship. I will never forget the day he apologized to me and said we were going to have to stop and get gas in his limousine. He went on to explain he never liked to have to stop at a gas station while he was transporting a passenger, but he received an emergency call just before picking us up, so we needed to fill up.

I told him I was enjoying our conversation and it was certainly not a problem as I would like to spend more time with him. We got off the freeway, and Ali drove along one of the city streets in a commercial area of San Diego. My colleague riding in the back of the limousine with me commented on the fact that we had passed several gas stations. When I mentioned it to Ali, he explained that he liked to go to the gas station a few blocks ahead of us on the right.

After we filled up with gas and got back on the freeway, I asked Ali, "What was so special about that gas station?" He laughed heartily and responded, "Well, there's probably nothing special about it except for the fact that I own it." When I asked him what else he owned, I was amazed at the long list of successful business enterprises he had created since arriving in the United States as a penniless refugee from a war-torn country.

I asked Ali how, as someone coming to America with no knowledge of business and unable to speak the language, he had become so successful. He laughed heartily again, which is his normal response, and said, "I learned entrepreneurship from you and business people here in America."

Never-Ending Journey

Many people mistakenly assume that entrepreneurship is a dog-eat-dog, win-lose field. Nothing could be further from the truth. As a fledgling entrepreneur, I called upon countless business owners for advice, contacts, and mentorship.

As you become a successful entrepreneur, you will want to help those coming up the same ladder behind you and smooth the path for future generations of entrepreneurs. The only thing that may be more exciting than my own success is to see those whom I have helped become successful themselves and begin to give back to still more aspiring entrepreneurs.

The journey of entrepreneurship never ends. You will always be looking for new ventures or ways to expand your current enterprise. Entrepreneurship comes in three basic forms. Some entrepreneurs improve on an existing concept. Others innovate and take the state-of-the-art into a new direction, and a rare few entrepreneurs invent or create totally new concepts that break new ground and go into areas previously unimagined.

If you are sitting with some friends at a local pub eating a hamburger and the thought pops into your mind, "I could make a better hamburger than this," you just had an entrepreneurial idea on how to improve on a current concept. Most businesses begin this way when an aspiring entrepreneur has the drive and determination to commit the future to the prospect of doing something better, cheaper, or faster.

Innovative entrepreneurs take existing concepts, but imagine new uses or new directions. I once consulted with an aspiring entrepreneur who had worked summers during college assisting a bricklayer. The bricklayer stood atop scaffolding and continued to build a wall as the young college student relayed bricks from the ground the top of the scaffolding. He told me it was exhausting, inefficient work.

Then one day, after a tiring eight hours on the jobsite, he drove home and parked his car in the garage. As he observed the electric garage door opener raising and lowering the heavy garage door, he had an innovative entrepreneurial idea. The technology designed to open garage doors could also deliver bricks to the top level of tall scaffolding where bricklayers were working. Innovative entrepreneurs understand that when you combine the right components with entrepreneurial vision, one-plus-one can equal ten or even one hundred.

Inventive entrepreneurs are the rarest breed. They imagine something that does not exist, and they bring it to the marketplace. They most often employ the thinking we discussed in a previous chapter that involves the fact that opportunities come disguised as problems. I will be eternally grateful that, in the process of losing my sight, I captured vison for my life. Sight tells us where we are and what's around us. This is a very important gift. Vision tells us where we could be and what is possible. This is an even more valuable gift. I am filled with gratitude that the vision I received, as I lost my sight, included the entrepreneurial invention of helping blind people hear what they couldn't see.

You will want to hone your observation skills and remain constantly mindful of the fact that improvement, innovation, and invention ideas are all around us. Carl Sagan said, "Somewhere, something incredible is waiting to be known." This wisdom is written in the heart and in the mind of every entrepreneur. Entrepreneurship is not just what we do, it is who we are, and therefore, it never ends.

A Larger Vision

Successful entrepreneurs don't work just for the money. In fact, it won't take long as you pursue your success journey until money is no longer an object. Financially independent entrepreneurs work because it's their passion, and they are pursuing a cause and a vision larger than themselves. During an interview with my great friend and mentor Steve Forbes, we were discussing the fact that we no longer work for money—we work for higher ideals. Mr. Forbes said, "You can't do nothing because nothing is the hardest work you'll ever do." He was pointing out the fact that rest, relaxation, and vacations are wonderful punctuations to our productive work, but they can't replace pursuing our passion and making a difference in the world.

Three of my greatest friends and mentors—Coach John Wooden, Art Linkletter, and Paul Harvey—did some of their best work after their 90th birthdays. Coach Wooden died a few months before his 100th birthday and was still creating value, providing service, and making a difference in the world.

A wise philosopher and theologian once told me that we need three things to be happy: something to do, something to love, and something to look forward to. Entrepreneurship can provide all three of these for you now and in the future. The journey of entrepreneurship often comes full circle and begins again, much like the cycle of planting, harvesting, and planting again.

Full Circle

As I described in a previous chapter, I went to visit my father, as my college graduation was approaching, to let him know that I was not going to get a job but, instead, I had decided to become an entrepreneur. My father's office was across the street from the Oral Roberts University (ORU) campus where I attended college. My dad worked for an umbrella organization that supported the university and other ventures around the world. During that fateful meeting with my father, he took me to the office next door to his where Lee Braxton worked. As I previously described, that became one of the most powerful relationships in my entrepreneurial life. Years later, as I was off building my various businesses, Mr. Braxton passed away, my father retired, and the university sold off that building.

Decades later when I met with the new president of that university and formed the Stovall Center for Entrepreneurship, he let me know that ORU was re-acquiring a building it had owned many years before, and he wanted me to consider housing the Stovall Center for Entrepreneurship in that building. President Wilson had no idea my entrepreneurial journey had begun in that very building forty years earlier.

Today, I have an office at the Stovall Center for Entrepreneurship in that same building. When my father and mother attended the ribbon-cutting for the Stovall Center for Entrepreneurship, my dad commented that it was only a two-minute walk from where he and Mr. Braxton had worked in that same building decades earlier. As I stood there, I was struck by the fact that my entrepreneurial journey had encompassed a two-minute walk that took me forty years of exciting growth, development, and success literally around the world.

Your entrepreneurial journey begins right where you are and will take you in untold new and exciting directions. In *The Ultimate Gift* movie trilogy, James Garner played the iconic billionaire entrepreneur I had written about in that story. As he describes success to his grandson, it mirrors my own journey in entrepreneurship. James Garner, as Red Stevens, proclaimed the words I wrote, "It's like going home to a place you've never been before."

CHAPTER TWELVE

Entrepreneurial Ecosystems

by Dr. Kevin Schneider

Perhaps one of the most grueling tests of physical endurance on earth is the Tour de France. With more than 3.5 billion television viewers and 12 million spectators, it is the world's largest sporting event, which has been estimated to be ten times bigger than any other race. There more than twenty teams that compete in the Tour de France with eight to nine cyclists on each team depending on the year.

The race covers 3,500 kilometers over the course of 23 days, and teams compete in a series of 21 stages. Over the course of the race, riders progress through a combination of flat, hilly, and mountain stages, and the most difficult stages include colossal summit finishes throughout the French Alps and Pyrenees mountain ranges.

Although a single competitor emerges as the winner of the Tour de France, it is impossible for any individual to accomplish this incredible feat without a tremendous amount of assistance. There is perhaps no other sport where such a wide range of support is critical to the overall success of the team.

For instance, the cycling team is comprised of riders who play different roles. Several riders compete for prizes and are identified by jersey color such as the GC leader[1] who wears the yellow jersey, the sprinter wearing the green jersey, and the overall mountain leader with the polka dot jersey. There are other roles, such as the domestique, who essentially supports other individual competitors on the team. Several of the members of the team can act as the domestique at different stages, and in doing so, this person sacrifices the opportunity to win a stage or compete for the yellow jersey.

As critical as a tight-knit, high performance cycling team is for winning the Tour de France, an even larger support staff with a range of resources is imperative. To support its cyclists, Tour de France teams may require nearly twenty additional staff members such as a general manager, mechanics, race directors, a technical director, a media team, hospitality staff—including a cook and even a doctor. This dedicated staff has a wide range of resources at its disposal to support the cyclists.

For instance, they often operate a fleet of vehicles including buses, vans, trucks, and several cars; dozens of bikes and spare parts; cycling equipment and specialized gear; and countless amounts of high-energy food and drinks essential for fueling the team as they collectively burn thousands of calories per stage. From the mechanics who ensure bikes are perfectly tuned each day to the chefs who provide nutrient-packed meals, it takes a seamlessly coordinated, herculean effort from the entire Tour de France team to emerge victorious.

Tour de Entrepreneur

It takes an entire ecosystem surrounding the tour de France team—including human, financial, and technical resources—to overcome the indomitable challenges and win the competition. Similarly, successfully launching a company is extremely challenging and may even seem impossible at times. Just when you navigate some difficult hills, you run into a mammoth mountain. Once you make it over the mountain and think you can coast through the flat plains, someone sprints by you. Or, you may be a great sprinter but fail to win due to a flat tire or bent rim.

Being an entrepreneur can be daunting with the wide-ranging scope of abilities required, seemingly endless hurdles to overcome, and ongoing risks and failures that occur. Like the Tour de France competitor, no entrepreneur can do it all. But the good news is that you don't have to; the entrepreneurial journey is not one you should travel alone. When you need support—and you will need it—there are more resources available today than ever before.

Entrepreneurship is a community sport, and entrepreneurial ecosystems are rapidly developing in both small and large cities in countries around the world. According to the Kauffman Foundation, an entrepreneurial ecosystem is, "A network of people supporting entrepreneurs, and the culture of trust and collaboration that allows them to interact successfully."[2] While entrepreneurs are at the center of the ecosystem, there are many important elements required for an ecosystem to thrive. Perhaps most importantly, entrepreneurs need talent to launch and grow their company. Like the GC contender on a Tour de France team, the entrepreneur needs a strong team around her that can specialize in areas such as programming, marketing, sales, operations, or finance.

Next to talent available in the ecosystem, entrepreneurs need access to capital. This can come in the form of equity or debt financing from angel investors, venture capital firms, traditional banks, or even state and government lending programs. Entrepreneurs also can raise capital through informal or nontraditional sources such as friends and family and crowd sourcing. Strong entrepreneurial ecosystems also provide access to other forms of capital such as knowledge and information. These resources may reside in fellow entrepreneurs, mentors and other professionals, or institutions such as universities, private foundations, and government programs. Resources can also include professional services such as legal and accounting, office space, and raw materials.[3]

In order for knowledge and resources to diffuse efficiently throughout an ecosystem, catalysts and connectors are needed who promote and bring entrepreneurs together to learn, collaborate, and challenge each other. These champions and conveners may be entrepreneurs themselves, members of a local chamber, or education leaders. Onramps and intersections are also foundational elements of a robust ecosystem. Onramps provide clear paths for entrepreneurs to get connected within the ecosystem and may include events like 1 Million Cups, organizations like incubators and accelerators, or economic development organizations like local chambers. Within an ecosystem, there are often many intersections where people, ideas, and resources converge which can include coworking spaces, meetups, and competitions. Whether human, technological, or financial, entrepreneurial ecosystems provide a resource-rich community vital for entrepreneurs to thrive.[4]

A Startup Community Near You

Development of entrepreneurial ecosystems, also known as startup communities, has become a global phenomenon. Startup Genome covers nearly 300 ecosystems globally, and the organization rates these communities based upon criteria including startup performance, funding, market reach, connectedness, talent, and knowledge.

As you can imagine, the top five global startup communities include the likes of Silicon Valley, New York City, London, Beijing, and Boston.[5]

However, there are also many lesser known, but rapidly emerging, ecosystems that Startup Genome tracks such as Mumbai, Kuala Lumpur, Estonia, and Istanbul. The emerging startup communities alone represent $348 billion in value and have produced 115 billion-dollar startups since 2010. As the startup culture continues to spread around the world and success stories and best practices diffuse across borders at an increasingly rapid pace, entrepreneurs in even some of the most remote reaches of the globe are gaining access to bourgeoning startup communities.[6]

In the United States, startup communities have become central to igniting economic growth across entire regions. In his book Startup Communities: Building an Entrepreneurial Ecosystem in Your City, Brad Feld describes his experience leading development of the startup community in Boulder, Colorado. According to Feld, the seeds for a successful startup community were planted long before the advent of the Internet. Technology, pharmaceutical, and natural foods startups were founded in Boulder during the 1970s and 1980s success stories including Exabyte, Synergen, and Celestial Seasonings. The University of Colorado's Boulder campus also played an important part establishing the foundation for the ecosystem. Today, Boulder has a flourishing startup community of successful entrepreneurs, seasoned leaders, VC and angel investors, a stream of young talent from CU, incubators, accelerators, planned events and organic meetups, and coworking spaces.[7]

While not as large or developed as Boulder, Boston, Austin, or Portland, there are many rapidly evolving ecosystems in lesser-known cities across the United States such as Salt Lake City, Omaha, Madison, and Charlotte. Tulsa, Oklahoma, for instance, is a mid-size city in the Southwest part of the US with a blossoming startup community. Tulsa sits right on Route 66—the historic "Mother Road"—once known as the oil capital of the world. While Tulsa may not top the list of the largest startup communities in America, it is a great example of a city in the middle of the country with a growing ecosystem. This is due in large part to great local leadership at every level from experienced entrepreneurs and investors to forward-looking city officials and generous foundations like the George Kaiser Family Foundation.

Once primarily known as a hub for energy, Tulsa is rapidly moving toward technology in verticals such as virtual health, aerial mobility, cyber, and analytics. Tulsa has a growing number of incubators and accelerators as well as coworking spaces, and state universities including the University of Oklahoma (OU) and Oklahoma State University (OSU); and local universities, Oral Roberts University and the University of Tulsa, are great feeders injecting new talent into the community.

Community: The Key to Wealth and Health

We need community for more than entrepreneurial success alone. Several studies demonstrate that community is as important for our health as it is for building wealth. In 1938, researchers began studying hundreds of male Harvard sophomores in what would result as one of the longest studies on happiness and adult life ever conducted. The research program followed the men for nearly 80 years with several of the individuals still alive in their 90s. Some of the participants of the study went on to become successful in business, medicine, and law while others ended up with mental illness or addictions. What the researchers discovered was that relationships have a profound impact on health. The study revealed that close relationships rather than money or fame kept people happier throughout their lives, and nurturing relationships is vitally important in addition to taking care of your body.[8]

As researchers studied everything they could find about the participants at age 50, the data consistently suggested that relationship satisfaction—not cholesterol levels—predicted which of the participants would be healthiest at age 80. Studies also revealed that marital happiness had a positive impact on mental health and couples experienced less mental deterioration as they grew older. The participants who had healthy relationships lived longer, happier lives than those who were lonely. In other words, studies found that loneliness is as powerful of a killer as smoking and alcoholism. The research further proved that relationship satisfaction in midlife is more important than genetics when it comes to healthy aging. In the words of one of the leading researchers, George Vaillant, "…the key to health aging is relationships, relationships, relationships."[9]

In his book *Outliers: The Story of Success,* Malcolm Gladwell recounts the story of a group of Italians from Roseto, Italy, who immigrated to Pennsylvania in the late 1800s. The town quickly came to life as the immigrants built homes, planted gardens, raised pigs, started businesses, opened schools, and established places of worship. A physician by the name of Stewart Wolf spent his summers on a farm near Roseto, Pennsylvania. During one of his visits, a local doctor informed him that heart disease was rare among individuals under the age of 65 in Roseto. This was during the 1950s when heart attacks were the leading cause of death of men in this age group. Wolf was intrigued and decided to take a closer look. After a lengthy, well-funded study, the researchers found that the men had far lower rates of heart disease and death compared the general population of the United States. Wolf initially thought that perhaps traditional dietary practices were the secret to their health However, when Wolf closely analyzed their eating habits, he found diet and exercise did not explain the positive health statistics as many people living in Roseto were heavy smokers and overweight.[10]

The researchers then turned to genetics to try to explain the differences in health. This too proved a dead end as relatives of the Rosetans did not share the same positive health characteristics. After ruling out diet, exercise, and genetics, the researchers realized that there was something inherently different about the community of Roseto. As they began to pay attention to the culture and ethos of the community, the researchers discovered that Rosetans were healthy as a result of the powerful social structure that made them resilient against the risk factors that were prevalent throughout the rest of the country at that time. This discovery challenged medical researchers to begin understanding health in terms of community rather than our genes and physical characteristics alone. Thus, the community in which we live not only influences our potential for success, but it can also have a substantial impact on our health.[11]

CHAPTER THIRTEEN

A Journey Ends and Another Begins

by Jim Stovall

You and I are about to end our journey within the pages of this book. However, your journey as an entrepreneur is just beginning and will continue throughout all the days of your life. The authors of this book want to continue to be your traveling companions on your journey. If you would like to receive my weekly column via email, find out more about the Stovall Center for Entrepreneurship, or just ask a question, you can contact us via jim@jimstovall.com or kschneider@oru.edu.

Although you are about to finish reading this book, your success as an entrepreneur is dependent upon the fact that you never finish reading. As a best-selling author of more than fifty books, I'm embarrassed to admit to you that when I could read with my eyes as you are reading these words on the page, I don't know that I ever read an entire book cover to cover. I read the minimal amount it took to get through school and nothing more.

After losing my sight, I discovered the National Library for the Blind, commercial audiobooks, and was exposed to compressed, high-speed, digital listening. I participated in an experiment to determine how fast listeners could hear and comprehend audiobooks. Over the years, I developed the skill of high-speed listening to a point where now, I listen to an entire book each day. Becoming a reader made me want to be a writer and also gave me the motivation, inspiration, and knowledge to become an entrepreneur which, in turn, has given me everything I ever wanted and more.

As we discussed previously, my own success and the lifestyle it has given me pale in comparison to the opportunity to pursue a higher calling and work for a greater good. While you may begin your entrepreneurial venture with the thought of making money to pay your bills and meet your needs, over time your thinking will evolve, and you will find that you are on a bigger entrepreneurial mission.

There are few things more sad than successful people who never look beyond their own gratification. These people suffer from the disease of "more," which is a never-ending struggle to acquire things that don't matter to impress people who don't care. Once you have met all of your personal financial needs, you then are in a position to learn what success, money, and free enterprise can really do for you and the whole world.

The "Brink of Failure"

Along your entrepreneurial journey, you will encounter bumps in the road, delays, and detours. Learn to look at them as opportunities disguised as problems. When Kathy and I first got the commitment from several small cable TV networks and a handful of independent stations to begin broadcasting our narrated classic movies, I thought we were on our way and nothing could stop us. Then, one of my colleagues who seemed to enjoy finding problems and dumping them on everyone, burst into my office and breathlessly declared, "Jim, we are on the brink of failure, and we're going to go broke and be out of business."

I responded, "What are you talking about? We have hundreds of independent stations and cable systems that are getting ready to air our programming in less than 60 days."

He haughtily replied, "That's exactly your problem. You've committed to hundreds of outlets to deliver two-hour blocks of programming via satellites at various times of the day and night, but our movies are too short."

I told him that we were getting ready to air some of the greatest classic films ever made, and he let me know that our movies averaged an hour and a half in length, and I had committed to delivering two-hour blocks of programming—so we were getting ready to have a half-hour of dead air on national television, and he wanted to know what I was going to do about it.

At that moment, I had no idea what I was going to do about it, but I knew that my problem-spreading colleague was not going to be part of the answer. In fact, shortly after that, I had to release him to go find an opportunity elsewhere. I have enough challenges with my competition that I don't need to pay teammates who revel in bringing me problems without possible solutions.

I told Kathy about our challenge, and when she asked what we were going to do, I said the first thing that came to my mind, "I'm going to host a talk show before each movie where I will interview the stars from the films." Kathy got out her big magnifying glass and we headed off, blind leading the blind, to our public library where Kathy found a book entitled, *Addresses of the Stars.* I wrote a one-page letter to some of the most iconic people in the fields of movies, television, sports, and politics. I told them what a great career opportunity I was going to give them to be on my mythical talk show on my currently nonexistent TV network. I closed by imploring them to contact me as soon as possible since we were going to be on the air the following month.

Opportunities Disguised as Problems

It was only ten days later when the first response came back to us in the mail. Kathy had her big magnifying glass and excitedly read the return address, "Katharine Hepburn, New York City." I knew that Miss Hepburn had recently turned down interviews with both David Letterman and Jay Leno, who were the late night hosts of the day, but I remained optimistic as Kathy opened the envelope. I remember thinking that, even if Katharine Hepburn turned me down, hopefully she had signed the letter, and at least we would have her autograph.

But she didn't turn me down. She simply wrote, "Please call and we can discuss the interview." I dialed the phone, preparing to talk with her assistant, her manager, or whoever else answered her phone, and I was shocked when Katharine Hepburn answered my call herself in that legendary Katharine Hepburn voice heard in countless movies. I was in shock speaking to her and blurted out the only words I could think of, saying, "Miss Hepburn, I'm surprised you answer your phone."

She was quite perplexed and responded, "Jim, don't you answer your phone? I've always felt when one's phone rings, one should answer it." That was the beginning of our conversation that resulted in the first interview on the Narrative Television Network. Getting the Katharine Hepburn interview for our first movie opened the floodgates; and in subsequent programs, I interviewed Frank Sinatra, Jimmy Stewart, Michael Douglas, and more than a hundred of the greatest stars from the golden age of motion pictures. Even within our entrepreneurial venture, one of our greatest opportunities came disguised as a devastating problem.

Guard Your Dream

When you declare yourself to be an entrepreneur and launch your business, a new group of people will enter your life. These people declare themselves to be "experts." They likely have no knowledge, experience, or expertise, but they will emphatically tell you countless reasons why your stupid idea won't work and how foolish you are to pursue it. If you believe these people, they become the most powerful individuals on the planet because they can destroy your dream; but if you don't believe them, they will eventually go away and bother someone else. Guard what comes into your mind and who you allow into your inner circle.

A big dream doesn't cost any more than a little one, but you can't judge the size of a tree from the size of the seed—just as you can't judge the potential of a business from the initial idea. Entrepreneurs are miraculous people who clearly see and believe in that which does not yet exist. The idea alone is little more than a legend, a myth, or a fairy tale; but when you take action, your dreams begin to become reality.

An ancient Chinese philosopher said, "Wisdom without action is useless, and action without wisdom is dangerous." Couple your dreams with knowledge, expertise, and wisdom, which you will have to borrow from mentors or books until you have your own knowledge and experience. Persistence is the crowning jewel in your entrepreneurial journey. Anytime you consider stopping along the way, you unplug your venture and derail your dreams.

I look forward to your success, and I appreciate the privilege of being a part of your journey. I will leave you with the words I share with each of my audiences at arena events and convention speeches:

Hold onto your dreams and stand tall
Even when those around you would force you to crawl.
Hold onto your dreams as a race you must run,
Even when reality whispers, "You will never be done."
Hold onto your dreams and wait for the magic to come,
On that miraculous day, your dreams and your reality
Will merge into one.

—JIM STOVALL

Notes

CHAPTER TWO The Entrepreneurial Mindset

1. Napoleon Hill, *Think and Grow Rich* (Meriden, CT: The Ralston Society, 1937).
2. "Entrepreneurial Mindset—An Entrepreneurial Learning Project," *ELI Mindset*, August 9, 2017; elimindset.com/entrepreneurial-learning/what-is -mindset/; accessed July 19, 2021.
3. "Entrepreneurial Mindset," *NFTE*; www.nfte.com/ entrepreneurial-mindset/; accessed July 19, 2021.
4. Simon Sinek, *Start With Why: How Great Leaders Inspire Everyone to Take Action* (New York: Penguin Business, 2019).
5. Napoleon Hill, *Think and Grow Rich* (Meriden, CT: The Ralston Society, 1937).
6. Napoleon Hill, *Think and Grow Rich*.
7. Ibid.
8. Stephen R. Covey, *The 7 Habits of Highly Effective People* (New York: Simon & Schuster UK Ltd., 2020).
9. "Intuition," *Psychology Today*; https://www .psychologytoday.com/us/basics/intuition; accessed July 19, 2021.
10. Galang Lufityanto, Chris Donkin, Joel Pearson, "Measuring Intuition: Nonconscious Emotional

Information Boosts Decision Accuracy and Confidence," *Psychological Science*, May 2016; https://pubmed.ncbi .nlm.nih.gov/27052557/; accessed July 19, 2021.

11. R. Buckminster Fuller, *Critical Path* (New York: St. Martin's Press, 1981).

12. David Russell Schilling, "Knowledge Doubling Every 12 Months, Soon to be Every 12 Hours"; *Industry Tap Into News*, April 19, 2013; https://www.industrytap .com/knowledge-doubling-every-12-months-soon-to -be-every-12-hours/3950#:~:text=%20Knowledge %20Doubling%20Every%2012%20Months%2C% 20Soon%20to,of%20Human%20Knowledge.%20A% 20transition%20from...%20More%20; accessed July 19, 2021.

13. Douglas Thomas and John Seely Brown, *A New Culture of Learning: Cultivating the Imagination for a World of Constant Change* (CreateSpace, 2011).

14. Carol S. Dweck, *Mindset: The New Psychology of Success* (New York: Random House, 2006).

CHAPTER FOUR Creative Capacity

1. David Burkus, *The Myths of Creativity: The Truth About How Innovative Companies and People Generate Great Ideas* (San Francisco: Jossey-Bass, 2014).

2. Tom Kelley and David Kelley, *Creative Confidence: Unleashing the Creative Potential within Us All* (New York: Random House, 2013).

3. Ibid.

4. Sir Ken Robinson, "Do schools kill creativity?"; Ted Talk, 2006; https://www.ted.com/talks/sir_ken_robinson_d _schools_kill_creativity/transcript; accessed July 19, 2021.

5. Ken Robinson and Lou Aronica, *The Element: How Finding Your Passion Changes Everything* (London: Penguin, 2010).

6. Michael J. Gelb, *Think Like da Vinci: Seven Steps to Boosting Your Everyday Genius* (London: Harper/ Element, 2009).

7. Madeleine E. Gross, Claire M. Zedelius, and Jonathan W. Schooler, "Cultivating an understanding of curiosity as a seed for creativity," Current Opinion in Behavioral Sciences, 35:77–82; https://labs.psych.ucsb.edu/schooler/jonathan/sites/labs.psych.ucsb.edu.schooler.jonathan/files/pubs/gross_zedelius_schooler_2020_current_opinion_in_behavioral_sciences.pdf; accessed July 19, 2021.

8. Amy Wilkinson, *The Creator's Code: The Six Essential Skills of Extraordinary Entrepreneurs* (London: Simon & Schuster, 2016).

9. Ken Robinson and Lou Aronica, *The Element* (2009).

10. Ken Robinson and Lou Aronica, *The Element* (2009).

11. Mihaly Csikszentmihalyi, *Flow: The Psychology of Optimal Experience* (New York: Harper Perennial Modern Classics, 2008).

12. Mihaly Csikszentmihalyi, *Creativity: The Psychology of Discovery and Invention* (New York: HarperCollins, 2013).

13. Mihaly Csikszentmihalyi, *Creativity*.

CHAPTER SIX Bet Your Beta

1. Kathleen Elkins, "Mark Zuckerberg shares the best piece of advice Peter Thiel ever gave him," CNBC, August 28, 2016; https://www.cnbc.com/2016/08/25/mark-zuckerberg-shares-the-best-piece-of-advice-peter-thiel-ever-gave-him.html; accessed July 20, 2021.

2. Doug Sundheim, *Taking Smart Risks: How Sharp Leaders Win When Stakes are High* (New York: McGraw-Hill, 2013).

3. Doug Sundheim, *Taking Smart Risks* (2013).

4. Amos Tversky and Daniel Kahneman, "The Framing of Decisions and the Psychology of Choice," *Science*, 211(4481), January 30, 1981, pp.453–458; http://www.stat.columbia.edu/~gelman/surveys.course/TverskyKahneman1981.pdf; accessed July 20, 2021.

5. Amos Tversky and Daniel Kahneman, "The Framing of Decisions and the Psychology of Choice."

6. Doug Sundheim, *Taking Smart Risks*.

7. Peter Sims, *Little Bets: How Breakthrough Ideas Emerge from Small Discoveries* (New York: Simon&Schuster, 2013).

8. Ibid.

9. Peter Sims, *Little Bets*.

10. Karl E. Weick, "Small Wins: Redefining the Scale of Social Problems," *American Psychologist*, 39(1), 1984, pp.40-49; https://homepages.se.edu/cvonbergen/files/2013/01/Small-Wins_Redefining-the-Scale-of-Social-Problems.pdf; accessed July 20, 2021.

CHAPTER EIGHT Learn to Fail–Don't Fail to Learn

1. Patrick J. Kiger, "6 Key Inventions by Thomas Edison," *History.com*, March 6, 2020; https://www.history.com/news/thomas-edison-inventions; accessed July 20, 2021.

2. Nathan Furr, "How Failure Taught Edison to Repeatedly Innovate," *Forbes*, June 9, 2011; https://www.forbes.com/sites/nathanfurr/2011/06/09/how-failure-taught-edison-to-repeatedly-innovate/?sh=14f4f01865e9; accessed July 20, 2021].

3. James Hayton and Gabriella Cacciotti, "How Fear Helps (and Hurts) Entrepreneurs," *Harvard Business Review,* April 3, 2018; https://hbr.org/2018/04/how-fear-helps -and-hurts-entrepreneurs; accessed July 20, 2021.
4. James Hayton and Gabriella Cacciotti, "How Fear Helps (and Hurts) Entrepreneurs."
5. Napoleon Hill, *Think and Grow Rich,* 1937.
6. Ibid.
7   "Entrepreneurship and the U.S. Economy," Chart 3. Survival rates of establishments, by year started and number of years since starting, 1994, 2015 in percent, April 28, 2016, *U.S. Bureau of Labor Statistics;* https:// www.bls.gov/bdm/entrepreneurship/bdm_chart3.htm; accessed July 20, 2021.
8. Steve Blank and Bob Dorf, *The Startup Owner's Manual: The Step-by-Step Guide for Building a Great Company* (Hoboken, NJ: John Wiley & Sons, 2020).
9. Alexander Osterwalder and Yves Pigneur, *Business Model Generation: A Handbook for Visionaries, Game Changers, and Challengers* (Hoboken, NJ: John Wiley & Sons, 2013).
10. Steve Blank and Bob Dorf, *The Startup Owner's Manual.*
11. Eric Ries, *The Lean Startup: How Today's Entrepreneurs Use Continuous Innovation to Create Radically Successful Businesses* (New York: Currency, 2011).
12. "How the CliftonStrengths Assessment Works," *Gallup.com*; https://www.gallup.com/cliftonstrengths/ en/253676/how-cliftonstrengths-works.aspx; accessed July 20, 2021.
13. Tom Rath, *Strengths Finder 2.0* (New York: Gallup Press, 2007).
14. Carol S. Dweck, *Mindset* (2006).

CHAPTER TEN Go for Grit

1. Angela Duckworth, *Grit: The Power of Passion and Perseverance* (New York: Scribner, 2016).
2. Angela Duckworth, *Grit.*
3. Angela Duckworth, *Grit.*
4. Angela Duckworth, *Grit.*
5. Angela Duckworth, *Grit.*
6. Caroline Adams Miller, *Getting Grit: The Evidence-Based Approach to Cultivating Passion, Perseverance, and Purpose* (Boulder, CO: Sounds True, 2017).
7. Angela Duckworth, *Grit.*
8. Jim Harter, "U.S. Employee Engagement Reverts Back to Pre-COVID-19 Levels," October 16, 2020, *Gallup.com;* https://www.gallup.com/workplace/321965/employee-engagement-reverts-back-pre-covid-levels.aspx#:~:text=In%202000%2C%2026%25%20of%20U.S.,far%20is%2014%25%20actively%20disengaged; accessed July 20, 2021.
9. Raymond W. Smilor, "Entrepreneurship: Reflections on a subversive activity," *Journal of Business Venturing,* 12(5), 1997, pp.341–346; https://www.sciencedirect.com/science/article/abs/pii/S0883902697000086; accessed July 20, 2021.
10. Xiao-Ping Chen, Xin Yao, and Suresh Kotha, "Entrepreneur Passion And Preparedness In Business Plan Presentations: A Persuasion Analysis Of Venture Capitalists' Funding Decisions," *Academy of Management Journal,* 52(1), 2009, pp.199–214; https://www.academia.edu/2245523/Entrepreneur_passion_and_preparedness_in_business_plan_presentations_A_persuasion_analysis_of_venture_capitalists_funding_decisions; accessed July 20, 2021.

11. Melissa S. Cardon, et al., "The Nature and Experience of Entrepreneurial Passion," *Academy of Management Review*, 34(3), 2009, pp.511–532; https://www .academia.edu/2877313/The_nature_and_experience_of _entrepreneurial_passion; accessed July 21, 2021.

12. Melissa S. Cardon, et al., "Measuring entrepreneurial passion: Conceptual foundations and scale validation," *Journal of Business Venturing*, 28(3), 2013, pp.373–396; https://activityinsight.pace.edu/mcardon/intellcont/ CardonGregoireStevensPatel-JBV-inpress-1.pdf; accessed July 20, 2021.

13. Steve Tobak, "What Makes a Successful Entrepreneur? Perseverance," *Entrepreneur*, January 25, 2016; https:// www.entrepreneur.com/article/269840; accessed July 22, 2021.

14. Pierre Azoulay, Benjamin Jones, J. Daniel Kim, and Javier Miranda, "Age and High-Growth Entrepreneurship," April 2018, *National Bureau of Economic Research*; https://www.nber.org/system/files/working_papers/ w24489/w24489.pdf; accessed July 20, 2021.

CHAPTER TWELVE Entrepreneurial Ecosystems

1. The general classification (or the GC) in bicycle racing is the category that tracks overall times for bicycle riders in multi-stage bicycle races. Each stage will have a stage winner, but the overall winner in the GC is the rider who has the fastest cumulative time across all stages.

2. *What are Entrepreneurial Ecosystems?* Entrepreneurial Ecosystem Building Playbook 3.0 (2019), Ewing Marion Kauffman Foundation; https://www.kauffman.org/ ecosystem-playbook-draft-3/ecosystems/; accessed July 22, 2021.

3. *What are Entrepreneurial Ecosystems?* Ewing Marion Kauffman Foundation.

4. Ibid.

5. Rankings 2020: Top 30 + Runners-up," *The Global Startup Ecosystem Report 2020* (GSER 2020), Startup Genome; https://startupgenome.com/article/rankings -top-40; accessed July 21, 2021.

6. Ibid.

7. Brad Feld, *Startup Communities: Building an Entrepreneurial Ecosystem in Your City* (Hoboken, NJ: John Wiley & Sons, 2020).

8. Liz Mineo, "Good genes are nice, but joy is better," *The Harvard Gazette*, April 11, 2017; https://news .harvard.edu/gazette/story/2017/04/over-nearly -80-years-harvard-study-has-been-showing-how-to -live-a-healthy-and-happy-life/; accessed July 22, 2021.

9. Ibid.

10. Malcolm Gladwell, *Outliers: The Story of Success* (New York: Little, Brown and Company , 2008).

11. Malcolm Gladwell, *Outliers*.

About Jim Stovall

In spite of blindness, Jim Stovall has been a National Olympic weightlifting champion, a successful investment broker, the president of the Emmy Award-winning Narrative Television Network, and a highly sought-after author and platform speaker. He is the author of more than fifty books including the bestseller *The Ultimate Gift*, which is now a major motion picture from 20th Century Fox starring James Garner and Abigail Breslin. Eight of his other novels have also been made into movies.

Steve Forbes, president and CEO of Forbes magazine, says, "Jim Stovall is one of the most extraordinary men of our era."

For his work in making television accessible to our nation's 13 million blind and visually impaired people, the President's Committee on Equal Opportunity selected Jim Stovall as the Entrepreneur of the Year. Jim Stovall has been featured in The Wall Street Journal, Forbes magazine, USA Today, and has been seen on Good Morning America, CNN, and CBS Evening News. He was also chosen as the International Humanitarian of the Year, joining Jimmy Carter, Nancy Reagan, and Mother Teresa as recipients of this honor.

Jim Stovall can be reached by calling 918-627-1000 or emailing Jim@JimStovall.com.

About Dr. Kevin Schneider

Dr. Kevin Schneider earned a Master of Business Administration (MBA) degree from Oral Roberts University and a Master of Science (MSc) and DBA in Strategic Planning from Edinburgh Business School. He holds dual positions as the Executive Director of the Stovall Center for Entrepreneurship and an Associate Professor of Strategic Management at Oral Roberts University.

In addition to the leadership and teaching roles, Schneider has advised startups and small businesses in developed and emerging markets during his tenure at the university. He has also led diverse teams in efforts to develop and implement global programs and social impact projects, and provides consulting and advice in the areas of business strategy and finance, leadership, and social impact.

In the author's current role with the Stovall Center for Entrepreneurship, his focus is on equipping entrepreneurial leaders to launch startups, scale small businesses, and impact communities.